HOLY DISRUPTION

Discovering Advent
in the Gospel of Mark

Tracy S. Daub

WESTMINSTER
JOHN KNOX PRESS
LOUISVILLE · KENTUCKY

First edition
Published by Westminster John Knox Press
Louisville, Kentucky

22 23 24 25 26 27 28 29 30 31—10 9 8 7 6 5 4 3 2 1

Book design by Erika Lundbom-Krift
Cover design by Marc Whitaker / MTWdesign.net
Cover art by Virginia Wieringa. Used by permission.

Library of Congress Cataloging-in-Publication Data
Names: Daub, Tracy S., author.
Title: Holy disruption : discovering Advent in the Gospel of Mark / Tracy
   S. Daub.
Description: First edition. | Louisville, Kentucky : Westminster John Knox
   Press, [2022] | Summary: "Presents a fresh understanding of the holiness
   of Christmas grounded, not in a conventional cozy Christmas message, but
   through Mark's disquieting gospel, which invites its readers to
   experience God's disruptive but transformative love for us and our
   world"— Provided by publisher.
Identifiers: LCCN 2022013451 (print) | LCCN 2022013452 (ebook) | ISBN
   9780664267384 (paperback) | ISBN 9781646982592 (ebook)
Subjects: LCSH: Bible. Mark—Criticism, interpretation, etc. | Advent.
Classification: LCC BS2585.52 .D373 2022 (print) | LCC BS2585.52 (ebook)
   | DDC 226.3/06—dc23/eng/20220610
LC record available at https://lccn.loc.gov/2022013451
LC ebook record available at https://lccn.loc.gov/2022013452

Most Westminster John Knox Press books are available at special quantity discounts when purchased in bulk by corporations, organizations, and special-interest groups. For more information, please e-mail SpecialSales@wjkbooks.com.

To Vic and Janet
and their example of steadfast love

To the Western New York congregations of
Central Presbyterian Church, Buffalo;
North Presbyterian Church, North Tonawanda;
and University Presbyterian Church, Buffalo,
whose educational ministries gave rise to this book

And to my husband, Timothy Wadkins,
whose encouragement and support
made this book a reality

CONTENTS

WHERE'S THE BABY?

IMAGINE IT'S EARLY DECEMBER AND, LIKE many folks, you head up to the attic to retrieve the Christmas decorations. One of the boxes you carefully open is the nativity set. To your surprise, you cannot find the stable with its giant star glued to the roof. Nor can you find shepherds grasping their crooks or any fluffy sheep to group around them. The box contains no regal-looking magi, no weary camels, no winged angels in long flowing robes. You are shocked to discover that the box contains no infant Jesus or his little manger bed either. "Wait a minute," you wonder. "Where's the *baby*?"

Turning to the Gospel of Mark at Christmastime is like trying to arrange a nativity set without the key characters. Mark's Gospel contains no story of Jesus' birth. There are no shepherds keeping watch over their flock by night, no heavenly band of angels announcing the Messiah's birth, no wise men who follow the star, meet up with King Herod, and offer gifts to the Christ child. Most significantly, there is no baby Jesus. Those characters that populate our nativity sets come entirely from the birth narratives in Matthew's and Luke's Gospels. Admittedly we are drawn to these nativity stories because in the midst of a very hard and harsh world, the babe is a gift of tenderness, hope, and innocence. Matthew's and Luke's birth narratives provide origin stories to explain the beginnings of this extraordinary man of God, this extraordinary man of love. He began as a baby, a gift of love wrapped in swaddling clothes. We can't imagine Christmas without the baby!

While the Gospel of John does not include the birth of the baby Jesus, it does provide a type of origin story for Jesus. John offers a *theological* explanation for Jesus' entry into the world. Describing Jesus as "the Word," John writes that "the Word was with God, and the Word was God. He was in the beginning with God." And then John offers his version of Jesus' birth when he writes, "And the Word became flesh and lived among us, and we have seen his glory, the glory as of a father's only son, full of grace and truth" (John 1:1, 14). John's Gospel supplies the fundamental theological meaning of Christmas, which is the belief that in some mysterious way, God became human in the person of Jesus. These passages about what Christians refer to as *the incarnation* are cherished Christmastime Scriptures and join the birth narratives of Matthew and Luke in providing glimpses into Jesus' origins.

In noticeable contrast to Matthew, Luke, and John, Mark offers no origin story for Jesus at all. Mark bypasses Jesus' birth and his child-hood entirely, makes no mention whatsoever of Jesus' father, and offers only a few passing references to Jesus' mother, Mary. Instead, Mark begins his account with a fully grown Jesus as he commences his ministry.

It could be argued that Mark's "beginning" story for Jesus is found at Jesus' baptism, where God declares, "You are my Son, the Beloved" (1:11). A case could also be made that Mark considered his entire Gospel to be Jesus' "beginning" story. Mark opens his Gospel by stating in the very first sentence, "The beginning of the good news of Jesus Christ, the Son of God," giving the impression that the entire sixteen chapters are but the start of the story of Jesus—a story that continues to unfold in the lives of Christ's followers even today. Nevertheless, since Mark offers readers no account of Jesus' origins prior to his official ministry, it might strike us as incongruous that we would have any use for the Gospel of Mark when celebrating Christmas.

Yet the Gospel of Mark does indeed have very important implications for this season of incarnation, especially if we understand Christmas not merely as the birth of the baby Jesus but more broadly as the coming of Christ into our lives and world. However, be warned! Like a jolt of electricity, Mark's message about the coming of Christ should absolutely shock us from our often complacent and self-satisfied lives. Mark will not permit us the soothing, sentimentalized Christmas our cultures have created from the nativity stories of Matthew and Luke, nor will it let us reduce John's incarnational message into a set of abstract and remote ideas. For Mark, the coming of Christ is a thoroughly countercultural event, disrupting our lives and calling for an inversion of the prevailing social order. The Christmases we construct for ourselves often amount to a kind of passive adoration of the sweet smiling baby in the manger—a reverence that romanticizes the child and asks little from us. In Mark, however, the incarnate presence of God comes in the One who challenges the status quo, engages the harsh realities of our world, and summons his followers to join him in a costly kind of commitment.

The Jesus we meet in Mark is edgy and

confrontational, a Savior who challenges us and upends the state of our hearts and communities. While Mark's Gospel will not give us a conventional cozy Christmas message, through this Gospel we can discover a fresh understanding of the holiness of Christmas—the holiness found when God's transformative love is born in us.

This book is designed to be a companion through the four weeks of Advent and Christmas Eve or Christmas Day. Each of the five chapters offers a reflection based on a different Markan theme and concludes with questions for group discussion or individual contemplation.

Chapter 1 explores Mark's idea of what it means to anticipate Christ's coming into the world. Chapter 2 examines what is really meant when we speak about the peace on earth that Christ brings. Chapter 3 focuses on our human longing for home and how God offers us a place of belonging in and through Christ. Chapter 4 explores Mark's unusual approach to the revelation of the Messiah. The final chapter examines Mark's concept of the incarnation, the hope we have in "God with us."

Mark gives us an unusual stack of gifts for Advent and Christmas: apocalyptic portents, open conflict, a new home filled with surprising relatives, a secret realm with its hidden Messiah, and the shadow of the cross. Such odd and disruptive gifts, to be sure! Yet sometimes the unconventional and unexpected gifts are the ones that bring deep meaning and lasting value. May your journey with the Gospel of Mark lead you to the Savior's abundant gifts.

Chapter 1

THE END OF THE WORLD
AS WE KNOW IT

Anticipating the Coming of Christ

As he came out of the temple, one of his disciples said to him, "Look, Teacher, what large stones and what large buildings!" Then Jesus asked him, "Do you see these great buildings? Not one stone will be left here upon another; all will be thrown down." (Mark 13:1–2)

"When you hear of wars and rumors of wars, do not be alarmed; this must take place, but the end is still to come. For nation will rise against nation, and kingdom against kingdom; there will be earthquakes in various places; there will be famines. This is but the beginning of the birth pangs." (Mark 13:7–8)

"But when you see the desolating sacrilege set up where it ought not to be (let the reader understand), then those in Judea must flee to the mountains; someone on the housetop must not go down or enter the house to take anything away; someone in the field must not turn back to get a coat. Woe to those who are pregnant and to those who are nursing infants in those days! Pray that it may not be in winter. For in those days there will be suffering, such as has not been from the beginning of the creation that God created until now, no, and never will be." (Mark 13:14–19)

"But in those days, after that suffering,

the sun will be darkened,
and the moon will not give its light,
and the stars will be falling from heaven,
and the powers in the heavens will be shaken.

Then they will see 'the Son of Man coming in clouds' with great power and glory. Then he will send out the angels, and gather his elect

from the four winds, from the ends of the
earth to the ends of heaven." (Mark 13:24–27)

"But about that day or hour no one knows,
neither the angels in heaven, nor the Son, but
only the Father. Beware, keep alert; for you
do not know when the time will come. It is
like a man going on a journey, when he leaves
home and puts his slaves in charge, each with
his work, and commands the doorkeeper to
be on the watch. Therefore, keep awake—
for you do not know when the master of the
house will come, in the evening, or at mid-
night, or at cockcrow, or at dawn, or else he
may find you asleep when he comes suddenly. And what I say to you I say to all: Keep
awake." (Mark 13:32–37)

HAROLD CAMPING, A CHRISTIAN RADIO
entrepreneur, predicted that the world would
come to an end on May 21, 2011. Through his
examination of Scripture, Camping arrived at
what he was certain would be the precise date
of the apocalypse, also referred to as the second
coming, when faithful Christians would ascend
to heaven and nonbelievers would be destroyed
in cataclysmic fires, earthquakes, and floods.
Camping spent two years proclaiming his

doomsday message, raising tens of millions of dollars from his listeners to pay for five thousand billboards and millions of pamphlets translated into sixty-one languages. As the predicted date drew near, Camping and his forecast captured the attention of millions of people around the globe. Some people abruptly got married, quit their jobs, racked up credit card debts, threw lavish parties, and, tragically in some cases, committed suicide. No one was more stunned than Camping himself when on May 21, 2011, the world did *not* come to an end.

Advent is the season when Christians prepare for the coming of Christ. Most of us, however, associate this coming with the birth of Jesus. At Christmas we sing "O Come, O Come Emmanuel" and "Come, Thou Long-Expected Jesus," anticipating the babe in the manger, *not* the catastrophic events of the second coming. Many of us would shake our heads in derision at people who are taken in by doomsday predictors like Camping. We don't believe such prophetic pronouncements, and we have little use for the notion of an apocalypse. But then what do we make of the Gospel of Mark, especially its troubling chapter 13? In this chapter Jesus *himself* talks about cataclysmic and cosmic disruptions and about the second coming of the Son of Humanity. How do we understand this unsettling pronouncement or the fact that Jesus is the one proclaiming the message?

The word *apocalypse* means "to reveal" or "to disclose." The term is associated with the unveiling of cataclysmic events, specifically those marking the end of the world and the confrontation between good and evil. While Mark 13 contains obvious apocalyptic traits, many scholars maintain that all of Mark's Gospel has an *eschatological* orientation—meaning that the entire Gospel deals with matters pertaining to the end times. This "end of the world" angle is most easily seen in Mark 13, which describes the disastrous events some believed would occur when God came to destroy the ruling powers of evil.

Biblical apocalyptic writings such as Mark 13, however, depict more than simply the end of the world; they reflect the belief in God's righteous *reordering* of the world. An ending, yes, but an ending followed by a new beginning and the establishment of a just and righteous reign. While the imagery is extreme, it was not necessarily intended to be taken literally. Rather, apocalyptic language was used impressionistically to convey the greatness of God's righteous intervention. Mark sees Jesus as God's appointed one whose intervention brings about the end of the world as we know it.

Chapter 13 is referred to as Mark's "Little Apocalypse," in contrast to the much longer apocalyptic writings found in the book of Revelation. Like most biblical apocalyptic literature, Mark 13 was written to bring hope and encouragement to people experiencing great tribulation. Those of us who enjoy comfortable lives of plenty will likely have a hard time regarding the end of the world as good news. However, for those people who experience great suffering and oppression, the end of their misery and the complete reordering of the world is regarded as something to anticipate and celebrate.

Mark wrote to a community facing such a situation. The context of Mark's Gospel is a harrowing story of unimaginable suffering. His Gospel was likely written around the time of the

Jewish uprising in 66–70 CE, when factions of the Jewish people rose up in revolt against the Roman occupation. The Jewish people greatly despised their Roman oppressors. Rome's excessive taxation on an already impoverished people fueled smoldering resentments. Hostilities also escalated due to various Roman indignities toward the Jewish people, including the command that they accept the divinity of the emperor and Rome's efforts to erect a statue of the emperor in the Jerusalem temple. Certainly Rome's notorious cruelty cemented the people's animosity. Severe reprisals followed any form of opposition. The commonplace sightings of crucified figures along the highways of ancient Palestine functioned to terrorize the populace into submission.

Despite Rome's military dominance, a segment of the Jewish people rose up in violent rebellion against this tyranny. However, not all of the Jewish people supported the insurrection, and the Jewish uprising against this foreign occupier morphed into a civil war. Some of the Jewish elite who served as collaborators with the Roman officials and who benefited from the existing circumstances fiercely resisted the revolt. Other more moderate Jews withheld their support because they did not believe the revolt was winnable. These internal divisions took a shocking turn when the insurrectionists launched a massacre against those in their community who opposed the rebellion. At one point, as the Roman armies were amassed around Jerusalem's walls, holding the city under siege, a group of radical Zealots tried to force the resisters to join their side by burning the city's entire stockpile of food in an effort to eliminate any kind of security blanket. Some records indicate that the resulting starvation killed as many people as later would the Romans. The ancient historian Josephus recorded the great deprivation within Jerusalem's walls during the siege:

> Then did the famine widen its progress, and devoured the people by whole houses and families; the upper rooms were full of women and children that were dying by famine, and the lanes of the city were full of the dead bodies of the aged; the children also and the young men wandered about the market-places like shadows, all swelled with the famine, and fell down dead, wheresoever their misery seized

them. As for burying them, those that were
sick themselves were not able to do it; and
those that were hearty and well were deterred
from doing it by the great multitude of those
dead bodies, and by the uncertainty there was
how soon they should die themselves; for
many died as they were burying others, and
many went to their coffins before that fatal
hour was come. Nor was there any lamenta-
tions made under these calamities, nor were
heard any mournful complaints; but the fam-
ine confounded all natural passions; for those
who were just going to die looked upon those
that were gone to rest before them with dry
eyes and open mouths. A deep silence also,
and a kind of deadly night, had seized upon
the city.[1]

When the Roman army finally breached the
last wall surrounding Jerusalem, its soldiers
unleashed a rampage of violence and destruction, burning buildings and slaughtering men,
women, and children. It is estimated that one
million Jewish people died in the revolt and its
aftermath. Thousands of others were seized and
enslaved. Then, in an ultimate act of retaliation,
the Romans burned down the Jewish temple,
a building that was not only a beloved house

of worship but was believed to be God's holy dwelling place on earth.

Mark wrote his Gospel either during or in the immediate aftermath of these disastrous events. The spiritual, psychological, and physical traumas experienced in the fall of Jerusalem form the subtext of his Gospel.

APOCALYPSE NOW

Those of us in the United States might recall our own emotions during the 9/11 terrorist attacks: our horror as the buildings collapsed, our shock in learning about the deaths of thousands of ordinary citizens and first responders, our grief, our fear. An apocalypse had occurred. These tragic events unveiled the scope of tremendous evil in this world as well as the deep-seeded rage aimed at the West and the United States in particular, shattering our national and our personal sense of security.

Another kind of apocalypse took place during the global COVID-19 pandemic. During the early days of the pandemic, as schools and businesses abruptly shut down, city streets lay emptied of pedestrians and cars, and the death toll reached staggering levels, many people exclaimed, "This feels apocalyptic!" The distress only deepened when we realized the prolonged nature of this apocalypse. The lingering virus thrust people into a world of unrelenting changes and losses. Suffering came in many forms during the pandemic: the grief for loved ones who lost their lives, the separation from elderly relatives, the anguish experienced by those who lost their jobs, the disruption to sacred occasions like weddings and funerals, and the stress that arose from the daily dose of unpredictability. In virtually every facet of our lives, COVID-19 brought an end to the world as we knew it and exposed our vulnerability to forces beyond our control.

For the Jewish people, the destruction of Jerusalem and especially the temple marked the end of the world as *they* knew it. Mark wrote his Gospel with these circumstances and emotions in mind. The turmoil of chapter 13 described not simply some far off *future* event; it also described the real-time apocalypse the Jewish people were *already* experiencing. Cataclysmic events had already occurred. These desperate people found encouragement in Jesus' pronouncements that he would come again and right the wrongs of this world. For Mark's community, therefore, the apocalypse was both a present time of suffering as well as a greatly anticipated moment of divine redemption.

In addition to the mass sufferings experienced from national or global events, Mark's Little Apocalypse prompts us to consider those smaller-scale apocalypses that occur in our personal lives that are no less devastating. What little apocalypses have you experienced that have brought an end to your world? Was it when you were served divorce papers? Or when the doctor gave you a frightening diagnosis? Maybe when your beloved spouse, child, parent, or friend died? Or when your boss delivered the news that you were being laid off? Or when your parents threw you out after learning you were gay? Or when you were injured in an accident?

A tragedy in my region brought into sharp relief how suddenly our personal worlds can fall apart. A local woman was walking her dogs in a wooded area when she was mistakenly killed by a hunter who thought she was a deer. The newspaper stories offered the basic facts. The hunter heard a scream after he fired the gun. He ran to the woman, applied pressure to the wound, and called 911. My mind, however, kept dwelling on those parts of the story that weren't covered by the newspapers and what I imagined took place: the hunter's emotions upon seeing the wounded woman, the frantic scene as he tried to stop the bleeding and called for help, and what I imagined must have been his desperate desire to turn back time and stop himself from pulling that trigger. In that fraction of a second, the world as he knew it, and that of his victim and her family, came to a tragic end.

Apocalyptic stories appear regularly on the evening news: airplane crashes, raging wildfires, oil spills. Spend significant time with refugees and you will hear stories from those who left everything behind in their flight from violence and took arduous journeys to find safe haven.

In these moments when we endure or witness such tragedies, we want a very big God who can do very big things. We desire a God who will intervene in our broken lives and world and make right what is wrong. Biblical apocalyptic writings give voice to this very yearning.

One such voice pleading for God to do big things was the prophet Isaiah, who cried out to God, "O that you would tear open the heavens and come down!" (Isaiah 64:1). Isaiah implored God to intervene in the injustices of our world in a grand and decisive way. Mark alluded to this Isaiah text when he wrote about Jesus' baptism: "And just as he was coming up out of the water, he saw the heavens torn apart and the Spirit descending like a dove on him" (1:10). Early readers of Mark would have recognized the allusion to Isaiah 64 and understood the implied message: God was now fulfilling the prophet's cry by coming down from heaven to reorder the world in the person of Jesus. For Mark's afflicted community, it was an answer to prayer.

I'll wager that you too have prayed for God to tear open the heavens and come down—maybe when watching particularly upsetting stories on the evening news, or when sitting beside the bed of a seriously ill loved one, or when confronted with the world's cruelty. Maybe your prayer sounded something like this: *O God, save my son from addiction! Heal me of my breast cancer! Stop the incarceration of immigrant children! Protect the endangered elephants! End racist police violence! Save my job!* Some of our prayers for God to "tear open the heavens and come down" are focused on the chaos we find *within* ourselves: our depression, our addictions, our out-of-control anger. Our outward and inward lives are in drastic need of reordering, and so we direct our prayers to our really big God who can do really big things. In other words, we offer our heartfelt prayers to an apocalyptic God.

EXPECTING THE UNEXPECTED

We must be careful, however, that we do not assume to know what that big thing will look like or when it will come. Jesus warns us in Mark 13 not to guess when or how God's reordering will take place. For centuries, people have scoured the Scriptures to determine the exact moment of the second coming and the form it will take. However, consider the thoroughly surprising way God entered the world in the "first coming": a vulnerable little baby born to an unwed couple in a backwater town who, when he grew up, was crucified like a common criminal. Who could have imagined that this would be how God would reshape humanity? God indeed entered our world in a decisive and powerful manner, but in no way did it match people's expectations. Jesus tells the disciples in Mark 13 to keep awake and stay alert because they might not be prepared for God's coming.

These warnings to the disciples to pay attention underscore that God's apocalyptic activity was not just a future event marked by cosmic upheaval but was unfolding right in front of them in the person of Jesus. Mark emphasizes that Jesus is the realization of God's radical reordering of the world. Jesus even used apocalyptic language when speaking about himself. In Mark 13, Jesus states, "Then they will see 'the Son of Man coming in clouds' with great power and glory" (v. 26). He makes a similar statement in chapter 14 after his arrest, when the high priest asks him if he is the Messiah: "I am; and 'you will see the Son of Man seated at the right hand of the Power,' and 'coming with the clouds of heaven'" (v. 62). Apocalyptic elements surface at the crucifixion: the darkness that descends at noon, the tearing of the temple curtain as Jesus takes his last breath. Mark includes these details to convey a startling message: in Jesus the apocalypse had arrived.

But what a most unusual apocalypse! God's confrontation with the world's evil forces is carried out by a messianic figure who makes himself vulnerable to that evil and dies a martyr's death. Instead of arriving like a superhero to settle scores with retribution, Jesus reorders the world by transforming his enemies with love and grace. While committed to bringing about "endings" to both personal and collective transgressions, Jesus' mission was not destruction but redemption.

Jesus sought to redeem individuals, often focusing on their physical needs. He healed people's bodies—those of the blind, the sick, the disabled—liberating them from their infirmities and restoring them back into the life of their communities. Jesus fed the hungry and raised the dead. However, Jesus' reordering of people's lives also included their inward conditions. He ate with outcasts and with despised tax collectors, signaling their worth. He forgave sins. He called people to repent. Through Jesus' love and mercy, people were set free from their guilt and shame, from anger and alienation, from greed and selfishness, and were offered a new way of living grounded in love and justice.

Jesus was also intent on transforming social relationships. When Jesus included outcasts, touched the ill and disabled, healed on the Sabbath, censured the religious leaders, and criticized unjust temple practices, he disrupted long-established social standards and set off waves of consternation among community leaders. Jesus' actions demonstrated a radically reorganized society based on forgiveness, compassion, and inclusion and embodied in a community where the least and the vulnerable became central members of the household of God.

When we look around the world today, it is clear that the reordered society Jesus spoke about is not fully realized. Jesus taught us what the transformed life in God looks like, but clearly humanity has not always paid close attention. Thus, we Christians find ourselves living between the two Advents: the Advent of Christ's first coming as a baby who grew into a man, and the Advent of the second coming, when God's redeeming work will be fulfilled.

Some Christians, like Harold Camping, focus their attention quite narrowly on the future coming of Christ, and their language of destruction and judgment can be quite frightening. While no one knows for sure what any second coming will look like, perhaps our best indicator for what the future holds can be found in recalling how God has acted in the past. In Jesus, God came in love. In Jesus, God came to transform, not to destroy. In Jesus, we discover a God who loves this world and seeks not its destruction but its redemption.

If God does not despise or reject this world, then neither should we. Thus, understanding the nature of God's redeeming activity in the world can redirect our focus from the future to the present. Those who live primarily for God's future intervention overlook Jesus' message that "the kingdom of heaven has come near" (Mark

1:15). God's reordering activity is happening now, in the present. And we are summoned to participate. Advent is indeed a season defined by waiting, but this waiting is not passive. In Mark 13 Jesus tells us *how* to wait. Jesus says, "It is like a man going on a journey, when he leaves home and puts his slaves in charge, each with his work, and commands the doorkeeper to be on the watch." Waiting means we are put in charge, each with our own work. We wait and watch for Christ to redeem our lives and our world by doing the work Jesus gives us to do.

There is a humorous poster that speaks to our human tendency toward passivity: "Jesus is coming; look busy." Of course, it's not just a matter of *looking* busy. We need to *get* busy with the work of God's kingdom: loving, serving, forgiving, exercising kindness, carrying out justice. An evening news program featured a group of doctors, many of them American volunteers, working to care for patients in Syrian hospitals who had become the targets of government fighter planes. Imagine the scene: bombs crashing into hospital wards, blowing up surgical rooms, landing on patients, killing the already injured. More than eight hundred medical professionals were killed by these bomb attacks on hospitals. When the doctors were asked why they would stay and serve in what was basically an apocalyptic nightmare, they answered that they saw this as the work they were given to do.

What is the work you have been given to do, even as you wait and watch for Christ to come into your personal pain and into our broken world? Where does God need you to forgive, to heal, to feed, to speak out, to hold a hand, to write a letter, to wash a body, to hold a baby, to stock a shelf, to march in protest? Maybe the work we are given begins with an honest reckoning of our own brokenness and a willingness to participate in Christ's radical reordering of our lives. Participating with Christ's transformative work requires a willingness to enter into the real-time apocalypses around us. In this world of violence, intolerance, and division, a world where global pandemics and the consequences of climate change threaten the welfare of our planet, God gives us a special task: being witnesses to hope. Faithful anticipation in the coming of Christ is found not in calculating the exact time of the Messiah's return, but in witnessing to his hope and love.

In Advent, we admit our longing for the coming of Christ to reorder our lives and our world. We admit that the world as we know it needs to come to an end. Hate needs to end. Cruelty needs to end. Suffering needs to end. The darkness found in our own hearts and souls needs to end. The good news found in Mark's apocalypse is that God does indeed come into our lives; God enters our pain, our brokenness, and our darkness to redeem us and our world.

Revelation, the big apocalyptic book of the Bible, ends with a three-word prayer: "Come, Lord Jesus." That prayer is a good way to understand all biblical apocalyptic writing— as a prayer for God to come and reorder our lives. It's an appropriate prayer for us in Advent whenever we open the newspaper, or turn on the news, or wrestle with our own little apocalypses. We utter this apocalyptic prayer of hope: "Come, Lord Jesus."

Questions for Contemplation or Discussion

1. The spiritual, psychological, and physical traumas experienced from the fall of Jerusalem form the subtext of Mark's Gospel. Think about modern-day widespread traumas. What effects have they had on people's outlook toward their world, themselves, and their understanding of God?

2. Have you ever experienced a traumatic, even apocalyptic, situation in which you called on God to directly intervene? Did you get an answer to your prayer? Was the answer what you expected?

3. What have tragic events that you have experienced—9/11, COVID-19, or other personal traumas—revealed or unveiled to you? What lessons can be learned from them? Did these events lead to any collective or personal reordering?

4. Can you recall a time when you chose to enter someone's apocalyptic situation and you served as a witness to hope? What difference did it make?

5. In Mark's Gospel, Jesus is presented as God's

intervention into the apocalyptic situation of Israel, but his entry into the world at that time did not fix the world as people might have expected. How did Jesus' entry not match expectations? What can the incarnation of Christ teach us about our own expectations for how God ought to intervene in our lives?

Chapter 2

PEACE ON EARTH, GOODWILL TO ALL

Faux Peace and Righteous Confrontation

Again he entered the synagogue, and a man was there who had a withered hand. They watched him to see whether he would cure him on the sabbath, so that they might accuse him. And he said to the man who had the withered hand, "Come forward." Then he said to them, "Is it lawful to do good or to do harm on the sabbath, to save life or to kill?" But they were silent. He looked around at them with anger; he was grieved at their hardness of heart and said to the man, "Stretch out your hand." He stretched it out, and his hand was restored. (Mark 3:1–5)

Then he began to teach them that the Son of Man must undergo great suffering, and be rejected by the elders, the chief priests, and the scribes, and be killed, and after three days rise again. He said all this quite openly. And Peter took him aside and began to rebuke him. But turning and looking at his disciples, he rebuked Peter and said, "Get behind me, Satan! For you are setting your mind not on divine things but on human things."

He called the crowd with his disciples, and said to them, "If any want to become my followers, let them deny themselves and take up their cross and follow me. For those who want to save their life will lose it, and those who lose their life for my sake, and for the sake of the gospel, will save it. For what will it profit them to gain the whole world and forfeit their life?"(Mark 8:31–36)

Then they came to Jerusalem. And he entered the temple and began to drive out those who were selling and those who were buying in the temple, and he overturned the tables of the money-changers and the seats of those who

sold doves; and he would not allow anyone
to carry anything through the temple. He was
teaching and saying, "Is it not written,

'My house shall be called a house of
prayer for all the nations'?

But you have made it a den of robbers."
(Mark 11:15–17)

On that day, when evening had come, he said
to them, "Let us go across to the other side."
A great windstorm arose, and the waves beat
into the boat, so that the boat was already
being swamped. But he was in the stern,
asleep on the cushion; and they woke him up
and said to him, "Teacher, do you not care
that we are perishing?" He woke up and rebuked the wind, and said to the sea, "Peace!
Be still!" Then the wind ceased, and there was
a dead calm. (Mark 4:35, 37–39)

NO ONE KNOWS FOR SURE HOW THE CHRIST-
mas Truce of 1914 began. Some accounts say
it was the German soldiers in their trenches
who first began to sing carols on that Christmas Eve. Then the British soldiers, huddled in
their own trenches, responded with some of
their own country's traditional carols. Back and
forth the two enemies sang to one another in the

darkness. When dawn broke, the German soldiers cautiously emerged from their trenches and approached their enemy. The British, observing that the Germans carried no weapons, nervously climbed out of their own trenches, and the two sides advanced toward one another in "no man's land." Accounts indicate that the soldiers exchanged small gifts of cigarettes, food, and souvenirs and helped one another retrieve their dead and wounded. More carols were sung, and some reports claim that the soldiers even played a game of soccer.

Such stories of peace and harmony are very moving, especially at Christmastime. Peace is an important theme of the season as we celebrate the birth of the Prince of Peace. Luke's Gospel reminds us that peace is a gift God offers us through the birth of Jesus. The heavenly band of angels announced the birth of Jesus to the shepherds, proclaiming, "Glory to God in the highest heaven, and on earth peace among those whom he favors" (Luke 2:14). In the birth of Jesus we recognize God's desire to bring peace to the inhabitants of earth.

This theme of peace envelops both the religious and the secular celebrations of Christmas. Decorative doves, the symbol of peace, hang as ornaments on our Christmas trees. A great many of our hymns and holiday songs speak of the peace that comes with the season. Our Christmas cards are adorned with serene images: the little town of Bethlehem bathed in gentle light, or snug snow-covered cottages with smoke curling from their chimneys. Television advertisements depict happy family reunions and laughing children. Our Christmas Eve worship services are designed to be peace-filled experiences with candlelight and tranquil songs. We want Christmas to be a season of harmony, and so we put a lot of focus on creating an atmosphere of peace during the holidays.

However, beneath the surface of this warm holiday harmony lies a great deal of wishful thinking. The realities of our lives do not typically match the peace-filled propaganda we find in the holiday images and messages. Instead of joy and good cheer, many of us enter holiday family gatherings with clenched teeth and knotted stomachs as we confront complex and painful family dynamics. Lasting family peace may elude us, and it is only a matter of time before we, like those British and German soldiers of World War I, once again pick up our weapons of anger, division, and hostility.

Even the peace we attempt to share within our communities at Christmastime is often superficial. The avalanche of charitable activities carried out by corporations, churches, and community groups during the holidays—the "angel" trees, toy drives, holiday food baskets—garner a lot of public attention for those few weeks but do not continue with the same vigor after the holidays and generally fail to address long-term economic needs. Some individuals, feeling the weight of their decidedly unpeaceful lives—their struggles, or pain, or loss—may drop out of sight altogether during the holidays, finding it too hard to pretend that all is well in their lives.

In truth, all is not well in most of our lives or in our world. Quite often the peace we attempt to create at Christmas is not genuine. It is a fake peace. Like faux pearls, or faux furs, or faux leather, sometimes the peace we settle for is a shallow imitation. We settle for this imitation because often we would rather accept a comforting lie than an uncomfortable truth. The comforting lies we tell ourselves are varied: maybe that our marriage is in solid shape when it is not, or that our children could never succumb to drugs, or that we don't have a problem with alcohol and could quit at any time we want, or that we can know security and happiness through the acquisition of possessions and the accumulation of wealth. Sometimes the lies that afford us a kind of faux peace are told to us by society at large: that lasting peace can come through military might and nuclear armaments or that our society affords equal opportunity to all our citizens. After the election of President Obama, many white people proclaimed that America had entered a "post-racial" era. This delusional belief permitted white America to continue ignoring the deep racial inequalities within our nation. These kinds of comforting lies permit us to embrace a momentary kind of fake peace.

This may last for a time, until the faux peace is disrupted by some event that forces us to face the uncomfortable truth—like the #MeToo movement of women breaking the silence around their experiences of sexual abuse, or the white nationalists' march in Charlottesville that exposed enduring racism, or the cases of police abuse of unarmed African Americans. The increasing frequency and ferocity of global natural disasters—fires, hurricanes, flooding—have finally roused some of the world's affluent nations into facing the reality of climate change. These kinds of events and realities force those of us who have swallowed the lies of the faux peace message to face unsettling truths.

A DEMANDING PEACE

Peace is an essential aspect of Jesus' agenda. However, Jesus radically dismantles the world's counterfeit version of peace to offer us that which is authentic and reliable. Ironically, we learn something significant about the Christmas message of genuine peace from the Gospel of Mark—a book that is, quite frankly, far from peaceful. In fact, Mark's Gospel describes a series of escalating conflicts that keep building right up to the climactic conflict of the crucifixion. At just about every turn in Mark's Gospel Jesus is involved in some conflict: exorcising demons, criticizing the hypocrisies of the religious leaders, and even clashing with his own disciples. Mark's Gospel is a tension-filled book in which the conflict keeps ratcheting up with each turn of the page.

It would seem contradictory, therefore, to claim that a book so filled with conflict could offer us a meaningful message about peace. Such an assumption may reveal our shallow understanding of the concepts of *peace* and *conflict*. Conflict is not necessarily negative or harmful. Conflict results when there are two opposing forces. When two countries go to war, we can easily see the harm inflicted by the conflict between those two opposing forces. However, in the civil rights movement people rose up to oppose the unjust laws and policies that oppressed millions of Americans. This kind of righteous confrontation was essential in the pursuit of genuine peace and justice.

The biblical understanding of peace was much broader than merely the absence of violence. The kind of peace called for by the biblical prophets, *shalom*, included the presence of justice and economic well-being for all. True peace was not possible where there was hunger or neglect, great disparities of wealth, or indifference to human suffering. Jesus stood in this prophetic tradition in calling for genuine *shalom*. The conflict we find in the Gospel of Mark arises from Jesus' unwavering commitment to the peace God intends for all humanity and Jesus' opposition to all the forces that threaten such peace—whether those are forces within us individually or communally.

What are these opposing forces? Following Jesus' baptism, Mark writes, "And the Spirit immediately drove him out into the wilderness. He was in the wilderness forty days, tempted by Satan" (Mark 1:12–13a). The word *Satan* in Hebrew, as well as the Greek transliteration used by Mark, literally means "adversary." This term occurs in the Hebrew Scriptures to refer to both human as well as celestial adversaries of God. By the time of the New Testament in the first century, Jews believed in Satan as a divine commander of the forces of darkness at battle with the divine forces of light. This adversary was believed to be the cause of much human suffering: physical as well as mental illnesses, natural calamities, and human sin and misery. Satan was understood as the great adversarial force to God's purposes on earth.

Jesus' wilderness temptation is his first conflict in the Gospel of Mark, and it involves confronting the adversarial forces within himself—all those forces that would tempt him to be something other than the one whom God called him to be. Unlike the Gospels of Matthew and Luke, Mark does not delineate the exact nature of Jesus' temptations. As human beings familiar with many adversaries within our own hearts and minds, we might imagine the nature of Jesus' temptations: the attraction of power and status, the selfish pursuit of pleasures and treasures, the pride and the fears that resist God's ways, the security sought in wealth, the behaviors and attitudes that harm others. The first confrontation Jesus has in the Gospel of Mark is with his own internal adversaries. What follows in the remainder of Mark's Gospel is the story of Jesus' confrontation with the adversarial forces active within the rest of us.

Quite often those adversarial forces that conflict with God's intended peace are manifested socially through the mistreatment and disregard of others. Mark tells a story about Jesus' encounter with a man with a disabled hand. Because of his disability, the man was considered unclean and was excluded from general society. Jesus desired to heal this man, but there was a problem: it was the Sabbath day, a day on which the religious rules stipulated a cessation of all forms of work. While exceptions were permitted for acts of compassion, the religious leaders in this story adhered to a very narrow interpretation of the law. Jesus knew they were closely watching to see if he would violate their conception of the law, and so he asked them, "Is it lawful to do good or to do harm on the sabbath, to save life or to kill?" But the leaders remained silent. Jesus "looked around at them with anger; he was grieved at their hardness of heart" (3:4–5). This is one of the rare passages of Scripture in which we are offered a glimpse into Jesus' thoughts and emotions: Jesus was *angry*, Jesus was *grieved* at the condition of their hearts. The leaders cared more about maintaining a rule than extending compassion. Jesus stood up to these religious leaders and their restrictive view of God's love by healing this man. The healing was a defiantly political act that disrupted the status quo of indifference, neglect, and oppression in favor of the expansive love and compassion of the kingdom of God.

How do our hearts harden in the face of human need, and how do the rules of our day— whether laws or merely social conventions— conspire to keep certain people oppressed? Much of the history of the United States is the story of discrimination against and exclusion of various groups of people and their efforts to secure full inclusion in our country's democracy: Native Americans, immigrants, women, African Americans, disabled people, LGBTQ people. Jesus confronts the adversarial forces of rejection, hostility, and discrimination that have shaped human history and that still infect our hearts and social policies. Instead, he calls us to live out God's authentic peace rooted in compassion and love. Jesus' kind of peacemaking involves more than simply good intentions; it summons us to action, to involvement. His version of peacemaking places demands on us and our lives.

In Mark 8, Jesus clashes with his disciple Peter after Jesus declares that the Messiah will be rejected, suffer, and be killed. Peter doesn't like this message. Like many of us, Peter was attracted to coercive power. He desired a Messiah who would exercise armed strength to overthrow the Romans and make Israel great again. Peter wanted peace for Israel, but a peace achieved through the same methods of domination that Rome and other worldly powers have always used to gain control. However, Jesus quite forcefully rebukes Peter and his false understanding of the Messiah's character and agenda. God's kingdom will not be won by replicating the systems and structures of dominance. Rather, God's realm will come through transforming this world through the supremacy of humility, sacrifice, and love. Jesus inverts the world's notions of how to wield power and how to achieve peace.

Then Jesus adds, "If any want to become my followers, let them deny themselves and take up their cross and follow me" (8:34). Being a disciple of Jesus means following him into the center of the world's pain—to where the "crosses" of hostility, resistance, struggle, and sacrifice are likely to greet us. Whether protesting social injustice, addressing issues such as gun violence or climate change, or advocating for a local immigrant family, pursuing God's peace involves confronting forces that oppose justice and compassion.

Most of us, however, do not like confrontation or conflict. We do our best to avoid such unpleasantness. Because Jesus taught us to love, we think being a Christian means being "nice." But genuine love demands justice. Genuine love demands confronting wrongdoing. Genuine love demands honesty about our failings.

In her book *I'm Still Here: Black Dignity in a World Made for Whiteness*, Austin Channing Brown confronts the Christian misconception about love. She notes, "Christians talk about love a lot. It's one of our favorite words, especially when the topic is race." She continues: "Love, for whiteness, dissolves into a demand for grace, for niceness, for endless patience—to keep everyone feeling comfortable while hearts are being changed. In this way, so-called love dodges any responsibility for action and waits for the great catalytic moment that finally spurs accountability." Brown writes of a different kind of love:

> I am not interested in love that is aloof. . . . I need a love that is troubled by injustice. A love that is provoked to anger when Black folks, including our children, lie dead in the streets. A love that can no longer be concerned with tone because it is concerned with life. A love that has no tolerance for hate, no excuses for racist decisions, no contentment with the status quo. I need a love that is fierce in resilience and sacrifice. I need a love that chooses justice.[1]

The Jesus we find in Mark's Gospel does indeed teach love. Yet his love incorporates righteous anger and confrontation.

CONFRONTING THE EMPIRES

One of Jesus' confrontational moments may surprise us: Palm Sunday. As we wave palm branches and sing uplifting songs in our

churches on Palm Sunday, few of us are thinking about confrontation or conflict. Yet conflict
is the subtext of the Palm Sunday story. When
Jesus rode into Jerusalem to the joyous shouts
of his followers, his procession was not the only
one taking place that day. Those greeting Jesus
as he entered Jerusalem to celebrate the festival of Passover would have been aware of the
other procession taking place across town: the
arrival of the Roman governor Pontius Pilate.
Pilate made it a point to come to Jerusalem each
year during the festival to ensure "crowd control"—so that the Passover festival celebrating
the Jewish people's liberation from a previous
empire (Egypt) would not inspire them to rise
up against their current imperial rulers.

In their book *The Last Week,* Marcus Borg
and John Dominic Crossan help us visualize
Pilate's arrival into Jerusalem:

> Imagine the imperial procession's arrival in
> the city. A visual panoply of imperial power:
> cavalry on horses, foot soldiers, leather armor,
> helmets, weapons, banners, golden eagles
> mounted on poles, sun glinting on metal
> and gold. Sounds: the marching of feet, the

creaking of leather, the clinking of bridles, the
beating of drums. The swirling of dust. The
eyes of the silent onlookers, some curious,
some awed, some resentful.[2]

This spectacle was not only intimidating; it
also supported an imperial theology. Support-
ers of the Roman Empire regarded the emperor
as divine, even referring to him as the "Son of
God" whose reign ensured peace on earth.

Now consider the contrast found in Jesus'
Jerusalem entry: Jesus riding into town on a
simple colt as onlookers waved leafy branches.
Mark's description of this event was intended to
prompt the readers to recall a passage from the
prophet Zechariah:

Rejoice greatly, O daughter Zion!
    Shout aloud, O daughter Jerusalem!
Lo, your king comes to you;
    triumphant and victorious is he,
humble and riding on a donkey,
    on a colt, the foal of a donkey.
                                      (Zech. 9:9)

Zechariah adds a description about what this
king will do:

He will cut off the chariot from Ephraim
    and the war horse from Jerusalem;
and the battle bow shall be cut off,
    and he shall command peace to the
    nations.

                (Zech. 9:10)

Zechariah's king ends warfare and ushers in peace. Mark's description of Jesus' Jerusalem procession, rooted in this text from Zechariah, prompts the reader to recognize Jesus as this king of peace. Borg and Crossan suggest that Jesus' Palm Sunday entry into Jerusalem was an intentional counter-procession to the imperial one taking place across town. This means that Palm Sunday becomes a face-off between two competing kingdoms. Through his counter-procession, Jesus confronts the faux peace of the empire with the genuine peace of God's kingdom.

We might regard Advent as a seasonal face-off between the realm of the true king of peace and the false realms of this world. It is easy for us to succumb to the myriad of social, political, and economic forces that offer false

conceptions of well-being. Yet through our celebration of Advent, we recall Christ's summons
to an unconventional way of being in this world.
Welcoming the way of Christ means turning
our lives, hearts, and priorities into a kind of
counter-procession against the "empires" of our
day. Consider the empire of consumerism and
its vice-like hold on most of our lives. Christ's
way of peace and justice stands in direct opposition to the dominant beliefs that one's worth
and happiness and peace of mind are found
through the acquisition of material goods and
wealth. How utterly ironic, therefore, that the
season celebrating Christ's arrival is marked by
a gluttony of greed and consumption! On Palm
Sunday, Jesus marched in a counter-procession
to the world's false empires and calls us to fall
in step with him.

Yet an edgy, confrontational Jesus does not
match the perception most Christians have of
the king of peace. Over the centuries, Christians
have tamed Jesus. We have tended to imagine
him as a mild-mannered, easy-going, rather
placid kind of guy. But Mark delivers a radically
different Jesus. In Mark we discover a Jesus who

assertively and vigorously confronts the forces that oppose God's peace-filled intentions for humanity. A prime example of Jesus' confrontational peace comes the day after Palm Sunday when Jesus enters the temple and drives out the money changers. This passage has greater impact when we imagine the details of that confrontation: the crashing of tables and chairs as Jesus flings them aside, the clanging of coins scattering across the hard floor, the astonished faces of onlookers. Nobody witnessing this scene could confuse Jesus for someone meek or docile.

What prompted Jesus' dramatic expression of anger? Money changers were a necessary feature of the temple, as many pilgrims came to Jerusalem from distant countries and needed to change their money into the temple's currency. Worshipers also purchased doves for temple sacrificial rites, a practice that may disturb our sensibilities today but that was a normal part of worship in that culture. Jesus' critique was not about the existence of the money changers or the sellers of doves but likely lay in the temple's exploitive economic practices that unfairly burdened the poor. Deep class divisions existed in ancient Israel between the small number of wealthy urban families who governed the temple in Jerusalem and the vast numbers of agrarian poor in the countryside. These temple authorities managed the collection of both religious taxes as well as the government taxes imposed by Rome. While virtually no one enjoys paying taxes, these temple-administered taxes were excessive and extremely harsh on the poor. As temple elites and Roman authorities grew vastly rich, many small farmers experienced a downward cycle of deepening impoverishment. Unable to pay the taxes, they were forced into debt, compelled to sell their land, and robbed of any means of survival. At the center of this injustice lay the temple. Jesus' temple demonstration was a symbolic shutting down of the temple's business of exploitation. We may recall 2011's Occupy Wall Street demonstrations, a contemporary protest with an analogous symbolic objective: to shut down business as usual on Wall Street in an effort to raise awareness of the systems of greed, corruption, and income inequality in the United States.

As Jesus overturns the tables he declares, "My house shall be called a house of prayer for all the nations. . . . But you have made it a den of *robbers*" (11:17; emphasis added). Jesus' words indicate that his objections centered on the problem of theft. The temple practices were nothing short of robbery of the poor at the hands of the powerful.

This story prompts a consideration of our own institutions of power—our Congress or our banking and lending institutions—and the ways these institutions' practices and policies benefit the wealthy and oppress people of lower income. Jesus faced off with the structures and people of his day whose unjust economic practices made genuine peace impossible.

Jesus repeatedly confronts the forces in society that thwart God's desire for authentic peace. He calls his disciples, you and me, and says, "Follow me." While most of us spend our lives trying to get along with others, the Jesus of Mark's Gospel reveals that conflict avoidance can be a failure in discipleship. Genuine peace is not achieved by everyone "being nice." According to South African Anglican archbishop

Desmond Tutu, "If you are neutral in situations of injustice, you have chosen the side of the oppressor."[3]

OUR PEACE PARTNER

The adversarial forces evident in human societies, however, have their origins within individuals. Each of us bears darkness and brokenness within ourselves that impact our personal well-being and our relationships with others. Thus, the pursuit of genuine peace begins with an honest reckoning of ourselves. After Jesus confronts his personal demons in the wilderness, he begins preaching to the people, declaring, "The kingdom of God has come near; repent, and believe in the good news" (1:15). Jesus' call to repent is a summons to righteous conflict with the opposing forces within ourselves that stand in the way of God's authentic peace: our self-destructive habits of overeating, overdrinking, overspending; our self-loathing as well as our excessive self-love; the ways we demean others in our thoughts and actions; the ways we accommodate injustice because we benefit from the status quo. Christ disrupts our faux peace with a message that cuts through our denials.

A friend of mine once served on a pastor search committee at her church, a highly educated and affluent congregation, where the committee's first task was to write a statement describing the congregation for potential candidates to read. After working diligently and thoughtfully, the committee submitted the statement to the church board for its approval. The board members, however, were distressed by one sentence: "We are a broken people in need of Christ's love." Broken? They were not broken people! They were among the city's most influential and highly respected citizens. The board members struck that sentence from the statement, believing it presented a negative and false representation of who they were.

In truth, however, we are all broken despite the size of our bank account, the level of our education, or the depth of our common sense. Any message we embrace about our worthiness that is not rooted in a recognition of God's love for us while we are yet sinners (Rom. 5:8) and our desperate need for this healing love is faux peace. Every one of us is wounded, lost, misguided, and subject to our cravings and fears. We cannot manufacture our own peace, although we do indeed try. We seek security, stability, and happiness through the accumulation of possessions, strong retirement savings plans, college degrees, home security systems, good careers, healthy eating and exercise programs, and a life of careful choices. Yet despite these efforts, chaos will nevertheless find us out. We cannot insulate ourselves from the myriad forms of chaos that can disrupt our lives—illness, death, heartache, divorce, estrangement, addictions, psychological and emotional pain—or the existential crises that can cause life to feel meaningless despite our "having it all." Burdens of the heart and mind disturb our inner peace with messages that we are not good enough, smart enough, or successful enough, with shame about past behaviors, and with deep anxiety about our lives and our world. Our efforts to find and to hold on to what we think of as peace in the midst of life's turmoil and the reality of our own failings, pain, and loss can overwhelm us.

What a relief that we do not have to confront our internal or external conflicts alone! We've got Jesus on our side! In Mark's version of the stormy sea crossing, Jesus and the disciples are in a small boat when a great storm arises, threatening the lives of all on board. Jesus remains asleep while the wind tosses the vessel and the waves engulf the boat. Terrified, the disciples wake Jesus up, saying, "Teacher, do you not care that we are perishing?" Jesus then rebukes the wind and the sea: "Peace! Be still" (4:39). And the storm is immediately calmed.

This story is much more than simply an account of Jesus' miraculous control over nature. The story demonstrates Jesus engaged in conflict with all the forces of chaos that would destroy our peace—both internal as well as external forces. It is significant that the Greek word used when Jesus woke up derives from the word *egeiro,* which is used later in the Gospel when the angel at the tomb tells the women that Jesus is "risen." It suggests that the stormy

sea crossing may be a foreshadowing of the resurrection, when Jesus will once again rise up
to confront the forces of chaos on our behalf.
We are not left to perish; Jesus has our back!
Christ stands with us in the storms of life, confronting the chaos of our lives and hearts and
bringing peace. It is possible that Jesus' command, "Peace! Be still," was directed as much
at the disciples' fear as it was at the storm itself.
Christ offers a genuine peace that no illness can
destroy, no failure can revoke, no hardship can
erase. It is a peace grounded in the love and
grace of God, who tells us we are worthy and
who offers us a more meaningful way to walk
upon this earth.

The Gospel of Mark *is* the story of Jesus
bringing peace to the world—not a sentimen-
tal Christmas feel-good story of peace but a
genuine peace that is hard won, involves hard
work, and is often disruptive to us personally
and socially. The world's faux peace may seem
attractive, but like the cheap imitation knock-off
products people sometimes buy, it is not built
to last. Only the costly but authentic peace of
Christ offers that which endures.

Questions for Contemplation or Discussion

1. In what ways have you embraced or settled for a fake peace because it was more comfortable or easier?

2. Jesus' Palm Sunday entry was a face-off between two competing kingdoms. If Jesus were to lead a counter-procession today, what empires might he be confronting? Name some of the daily confrontations you encounter between the fake peace of the empire and the genuine peace of God's kingdom.

3. What competing empires do we encounter during the holiday season? Where do you see evidence of Christians resisting or succumbing to these forces?

4. What difference does it make to your understanding of Jesus and to your personal faith to think of Jesus as a countercultural disrupter of the status quo?

5. How might Jesus' concept of peace change how you celebrate Christmas?

Chapter 3

HOME FOR THE HOLIDAYS

Finding Our Home in the Kingdom of God

Now after John was arrested, Jesus came to Galilee, proclaiming the good news of God, and saying, "The time is fulfilled, and the kingdom of God has come near; repent, and believe in the good news." (Mark 1:14–15)

Then his mother and his brothers came; and standing outside, they sent to him and called him. A crowd was sitting around him; and they said to him, "Your mother and your brothers and sisters are outside, asking for you." And he replied, "Who are my mother and my brothers?" And looking at those who sat around him, he said, "Here are my mother and my brothers! Whoever does the will of God is my brother and sister and mother." (Mark 3:31–35)

People were bringing little children to him in order that he might touch them; and the disciples spoke sternly to them. But when Jesus saw this, he was indignant and said to them, "Let the little children come to me; do not stop them; for it is to such as these that the kingdom of God belongs. Truly I tell you, whoever does not receive the kingdom of God as a little child will never enter it." And he took them up in his arms, laid his hands on them, and blessed them. (Mark 10:13–16)

One of the scribes came near and heard them disputing with one another, and seeing that he answered them well, he asked him, "Which commandment is the first of all?" Jesus answered, "The first is, 'Hear, O Israel: the Lord our God, the Lord is one; you shall love the Lord your God with all your heart, and with all your soul, and with all your mind, and with all your strength.' The second is this,

'You shall love your neighbor as yourself.'
There is no other commandment greater than
these." Then the scribe said to him, "You are
right, Teacher; you have truly said that 'he is
one, and besides him there is no other'; and
'to love him with all the heart, and with all
the understanding, and with all the strength',
and 'to love one's neighbor as oneself'—this
is much more important than all whole burnt
offerings and sacrifices." When Jesus saw that
he answered wisely, he said to him, "You are
not far from the kingdom of God." After that
no one dared to ask him any question. (Mark
12:28–34)

THE WIZARD OF OZ, THE MUCH-LOVED CLAS-
sic movie, tells the story of a young girl, Dorothy, who is transported to the fantastical world
of Oz and, together with three new friends,
endeavors to find her way back home. Their
unfolding odyssey of adventures, dangers, and
obstacles in pursuit of this goal turns this story
into a metaphor of the *human* story. Home is
the cherished destination for all of us in our
journeys through life. We long to find that place
of belonging where we are accepted, loved,
and safe.

Our concept of home is often geographically grounded. Humans have always carved out territories they claim as their home and have fought and died defending these places from others. Far from their homeland, immigrants hold tight to customs and foods that make them feel at home. I grew up in the Arizona desert surrounding Tucson. This place will always feel like home no matter how many years I live elsewhere. However, the qualities of my homeland that are precious to me—the giant saguaro cactus, the craggy mountains framed against the cobalt sky, the fragrance of creosote bushes, the raspy call of the cactus wren—baffle my husband, who finds the landscape harsh and barren. He grew up in California and misses the coast, where the waves crash on the shore and the air tastes of salt.

Our concept of home is more than a physical place, however. The feeling of home is often fostered by the emotional connections we develop with the people and culture of a place and our shared experiences with others. In my adopted home of Buffalo, New York, residents have a deep cultural bond with one another forged in part through the shared history of economic struggle and revival, the actions of good neighbors during many blizzards, and the pride and pain in its sports teams. Some families have resided in the same neighborhood for generations, and the emotional and social connections within extended families as well as among neighbors is strong.

No other season of the year extols the blessings of home quite like Christmas. Social messages promote a focus on home as the essential ingredient in the celebration of the holiday. As one of the most heavily traveled times of the year, we witness the great effort and expense people make to be where the geographical and emotional bonds of home unite. When Bing Crosby or Perry Como croon their holiday classics, "I'll Be Home for Christmas" or "(There's No Place Like) Home for the Holidays," they elicit yearnings to spend the season in that place where we feel most secure and loved. And the underlying sentiment in these songs is a longing to feel at home during the remainder of the year as well.

And yet as a destination, home is elusive.

Some of us may not have enjoyed a happy childhood home. Others experience pain and conflict in their current home. Maybe our sense of home was lost to us when a loved one died or when a life partner walked away from the relationship. As members of a highly mobile society, our original home may lie on the other side of the country or even the globe. Perhaps we cannot return home because the place we call home is simply no longer there—destroyed in a fire or torn down to make way for a shopping center. We learn with tragic frequency about entire communities that have suffered from disasters—fires, earthquakes, hurricanes, tornados, even volcanoes—that have resulted in the total destruction of their homes. Even individuals who enjoy settled lives, social acceptance, and economic well-being may experience an existential longing for home. Confronted with feelings of meaninglessness ("What's the point of my life?") and insignificance, they grasp for ways to feel whole. They marry a person thinking he or she will fill their longing for home. They have children in hopes they will provide a sense of home. They fill their houses with beautiful possessions to feel at home. Yet the sense of home may still be elusive. Overcome by emptiness and alienation, many turn to destructive behaviors to dull the pain of its absence.

Norma, one of the elderly members of my congregation, lived all of her ninety-one years in the same house. Norma was adamant that even in her declining health she wanted to remain in her home. As she lived alone and had no living relatives, the members of the church stepped in and did their best to fulfill Norma's desire— taking her to medical appointments, managing her finances, checking on her, and arranging for home-care professionals to assist her with daily living. When a health emergency sent Norma to the hospital, however, it became evident that her medical condition would not permit her to return home. This news devastated her. Church members did their best to help Norma transition to her care facility, regularly visiting her there during those final six months of her life. But Norma never adjusted to her new residence. In the last conversation I had with her at the hospice unit two days before her death, she was bedridden, on oxygen, and barely able to talk, but she turned to me and asked, "Could you take me home?" It was heartbreaking to confess to her that I was not capable of fulfilling this desire.

It *is* heartbreaking to consider the myriad people in our country and across the globe who are denied both a physical home or the sense of belonging. Everyone has a right to a home. But every year millions of Americans are forced from their homes. Author Matthew Desmond chronicles in his book *Evicted* the lives of eight low-income Milwaukee families who endure the trauma of repeated evictions. What Desmond calls the "violence of displacement" has deep and lasting repercussions, affecting the physical and mental health of families, destabilizing the lives of the children as they are pulled in and out of schools, and exacting a heavy toll on entire neighborhoods.[1]

The idea of homelessness has a deep historical dimension. During the more than two hundred years when millions of people were ripped away from their homes in Africa and sold into slavery, and well beyond the time slavery ended, African Americans were not afforded equal rights, privileges, or social acceptance. Systemic forms of racism, such as Jim Crow laws and red-lining in the real estate market, legally codified discrimination in order to erect barriers to African American educational opportunities and economic prosperity. The message in these forms of bias was clear: "You do not belong. This is not your home."

In her book *White Fragility: Why It's So Hard for White People to Talk about Racism*, Robin DiAngelo reflects on the privileged assumption of belonging that white people like herself take for granted:

> As I move through my daily life, my race is unremarkable. I belong when I turn on the TV, read best-selling novels, and watch blockbuster movies. I belong when I walk past the magazine racks at the grocery store or drive past billboards. . . . I belong when I look at my teachers, counselors, and classmates. I belong when I learn about the history of my country throughout the year and when I am shown its heroes and heroines. . . . I belong when I speak to my children's teachers, when I talk to their camp counselors, when I consult with their doctors and dentists. . . . In virtually every situation or context deemed normal, neutral or

prestigious in society, I belong racially. This belonging is a deep and ever-present feeling that has always been with me.[2]

Many African Americans experience a starkly different reality. Underrepresented in upper levels of employment and politics as well as in film, television, and magazines, African Americans maneuver daily through a society where whiteness is normative. Unlike DiAngelo, many African Americans do not experience a "deep and ever-present feeling" of belonging.

THE DISPLACED PEOPLE OF GOD

The Jewish people of the Bible understood this yearning for home. The two most pivotal events in Jewish biblical history, the exodus and the exile, revolve around the theme of home. After escaping their enslavement in Egypt, the Jewish people, guided by Moses, wandered for forty years in the wilderness in search of their new home, the promised land. The exodus was a time of great longing, doubting, and then renewing of their trust in God's promise to lead them to a place of well-being and prosperity. Their quest for home finally came to an end when they settled in the promised land of Canaan.

That joyous "homecoming," however, was also accompanied by tragedy and displacement when these new arrivals to Canaan violently expelled the inhabitants of that land. This kind of tragic confrontation between those seeking a homeland and those affected by that quest has played out repeatedly in human history: the Puritans' arrival in North America and the disastrous consequences for Native Americans, the tensions surrounding contemporary migrants and refugees seeking asylum in other nations, the conflict regarding homeland in the Middle East. Often the human quest for home is fraught with political, social, and ethical complexities as well as profound transgressions against others.

Some seven hundred years after the exodus, the Jewish people suffered another crisis related to "home." The exile occurred after the Jewish people were conquered by the Babylonian army and a sizeable portion of the citizens were forced from their cherished homeland to live in exile in Babylon. This was a time when

the Jewish people experienced intense home-
sickness. Some of the most beloved writings
from the biblical prophets speak words of comfort to the exiled people, assuring them that
God would indeed deliver them home one day.
When the Jewish people were finally released
from their captivity and allowed to return home,
they discovered a greatly altered homeland in
need of much rebuilding. Life did not just pick
up where it had left off; home had to be rebuilt
with time and effort. This is fundamentally true
for all of us when our sense of home has broken
down—in times of grief and loss, after the rup-
ture of a relationship, or when the trust between
groups of people is destroyed. It takes effort,
time, and intentionality to create a new sense of
well-being.

The Jewish people of Jesus' day lived with
this historic memory of seeking, finding, losing,
grieving for, and re-creating home. Furthermore,
at the time of Jesus' birth, the Jewish homeland was once again under the domination of
a foreign power—the Roman Empire—which
robbed the Jews of an emotional, spiritual, and
psychological sense of well-being and security.

Into this situation of displacement, Jesus is born. The Christmas story of his birth is the celebration of God bringing all people a precious gift: the gift of home. One of Christianity's cherished Christmastime texts comes from the Gospel writer John, who refers to Jesus as "the Word" and states, "And the Word became flesh and lived among us" (John 1:14). The Greek phrase that appears in the New Revised Standard Version as "lived among us" literally translates to "pitched a tent among us." Thus, we can understand Christmas as the celebration of God's coming to set up a home, a tent of sorts, with us and for us. God throws open the tent flap and invites us to enter. The coming of Jesus into our lives offers us a home of meaning, belonging, and acceptance that accompanies us—just like a tent— wherever life's journey takes us. Home is found in Jesus and his way.

While the Gospel of Mark lacks the nostalgic Christmas narratives we so cherish, it does capture the theme of home through its focus on the kingdom of God. Unlike earthly kingdoms, this realm is not defined by geography but refers to the home we can find in God and the home

God desires to establish in us. Jesus' very first words in Mark are about this special home. Mark writes, "Jesus came to Galilee, proclaiming the good news of God, and saying, 'The time is fulfilled, and the kingdom of God has come near; repent and believe in the good news'" (1:14–15). Mark wants us to understand that Jesus' arrival ushers in this kingdom of God. Jesus comes into our lives with the expressed purpose of helping us find our way to this special home.

ENLARGING THE HOME

What is this kingdom of God like? For the Gospel writer, Jesus not only ushers in God's kingdom, but Jesus *embodies* God's kingdom. This means that when we look at Jesus, at what he does and what he says, we learn what the kingdom of God is like. And quite often we are shocked by what Jesus reveals about God's household.

Take, for instance, the concept of the family. The notion of home is usually associated with the bonds of kinship. Yet when Jesus is told that his mother and brothers and sisters are outside waiting to see him, he responds by declaring, "Who are my mother and my brothers?" Then he adds, "Whoever does the will of God is my brother and sister and mother" (3:33). This was a radical statement in a society in which kinship was the foundational entity of belonging. To those listening to Jesus, it would seem as if he were devaluing the most important structure of society. His pronouncement is not easy on our ears either. We live in a culture where the phrase "Family first" is a common sentiment used to express our deepest allegiances.

Jesus' proclamation, however, was not intended to devalue families. In fact, he was offering an expanded concept of home and kinship. Jesus proposed that our ultimate and most secure place of belonging is found not in the important but flawed institution of the family, but rather in the household of God and its values. The prevailing notion of family based on bloodlines is simply too narrow for the values of the kingdom of God. Imagine how shocked, even threatened, people must have felt to hear Jesus blur the boundaries of kinship. Family allegiances formed the economic and social

foundations of their society, and they deter-
mined such matters as the inheritance of property and those whom one was obligated to
protect and support. What might it mean for
society if anybody could be considered family?
The implications of this question were and are
still today deeply disrupting to the status quo.

What makes Jesus' proclamation about the
family especially radical is the way he expanded
the circle of preference to include a scandalous
assortment of society's least respected people.
When Jesus touched lepers, healed the blind and
the sick, ate with tax collectors, and included
women, he transgressed the conventional social
boundaries erected by his culture. His shocking behavior demonstrated that the kingdom of
God includes every kind of person, especially
those most excluded, and that compassion and
acceptance are core features of the household
of God.

Gordon Light's song "Draw the Circle
Wide" speaks to this kind of inclusion:

Draw the circle wide, draw it wider still,
Let this be our song: no one stands alone

standing side by side.
Draw the circle wide.[3]

The idea of "family first" narrows the circle of belonging to a select few. Historically, this is what humans have always done, narrowing the circle of belonging around clan or nation, race or gender, class standing or sexual orientation, the cool kids' table or the first-class lounge. Jesus demonstrates that the kingdom of God expands the circle of who is accepted, of who is allowed in, of who can find a home in the love of God. Thus, Jesus not only offers us a new home, but he gives us a new family—a whole new assembly of "relatives" who all reside under the same roof of God's love.

THE FAMILY APPROACHES the baptismal font with their infant daughter. Cradling the child in her arms, the pastor dips her hand into the water and lays it on the child's head, announcing, "Maya Elizabeth, I baptize you in the name of the Father, and of the Son, and of the Holy Spirit." When I was growing up, I often wondered why the pastors of the Protestant churches I attended declared the individual's first and middle names but never used the person's last name in the sacrament of baptism. What was up with that? Only much later did it dawn on me that our last names represent our *family* name: the Greens, the Patels, the Johnsons, the Kims. These last names identify the group of people to whom we belong. In baptism, however, we are welcomed into *God's* family. Our identity is rooted in the household of God. One could say that in baptism we are given a new "last" name. The story of Jesus' baptism when God declared, "You are my Son, the Beloved," suggests our new last name: God's beloved.

Every one of us has been claimed by God as beloved. We have been welcomed home. Of course, we will mess up. We will fail and fall short of who we were created to be. Yet God's grace, God's deep well of kindness, love, and forgiveness will always be extended to us. The message found in Jesus' life, death, and resurrection is that we are loved and accepted by God *while we are yet sinners*. As the children's song taught us, "Jesus loves me this I know, for the Bible tells me so." We are assured a place of belonging in the heart of God. What profound comfort this assurance offers to all who know the brokenness of internal as well as external homes!

Next comes the challenging part, the part that is often hard for us to accept and live out. Because baptism does not bestow God's love on us but rather *acknowledges* the love that is *already* present from the moment of our creation, every person we meet, regardless of ethnicity, religion, age, income, sexual orientation, race, or any other circumstance or condition is also *God's beloved*. They are family. Being baptized into Christ means we follow Jesus on the way of inclusive love.

It is evident from his ministry that Jesus was not only concerned with people having a heavenly home but also with their having a place of well-being during their lives on earth. Yet we live in a world that far too often denies people a home—both a physical as well as an emotional home—and tells them they are unwanted and do not belong. Public health studies document that the suicide rates among LGBTQ youth are substantially higher than among cisgender, heterosexual youth. Rejected by family, classmates, and the wider community, subject to intense bullying, and lacking safe and supportive places, many LGBTQ youth are overwhelmed by feelings of alienation. Religious communities also play a role in this alienation. One study indicates a correlation between LGBTQ youth who hold strong religious beliefs and an increase in suicidal thoughts and action—whereas heterosexual youth with strong religious engagement demonstrate a lower frequency of suicidal thoughts and behaviors.[4] While there are indeed religious communities supportive of sexual minorities, far too many LGBTQ youth find themselves in conflict with a religious tradition that does not affirm who they are or their right to participate in that faith community.

Those of us baptized into the household of God are called to demonstrate Christ's own inclusive love. Baptism not only tells us *whose* we are (God's beloved and members of God's household) but also tells us *who* we are: followers of Jesus. After his baptism, Jesus went forth to teach and model what it looks like to be a member of God's household. Members of God's family extend love, offer compassion, care for the vulnerable, and work to forgive. Adolescents heading out the door for an evening with friends might be told by their parents, "Remember who you are." It is a gentle reminder to a youth to recall the values that the family has imparted. So it is with baptism. In our daily lives, we are invited to recall our baptism and who we are as members of God's household and as followers of the homeland of Jesus. And then we are to conduct ourselves accordingly. Thus, God's home both *claims* us as well as *shapes* us.

Jesus' followers had a hard time understanding his message of radical inclusion. More than once, Mark shares stories of the disciples jockeying for positions of status and privilege. Mark tells the story of people who brought children to Jesus for him to bless and how the disciples tried to shoo them away. Children were the least powerful members of society and occupied the

lowest rung on the social ladder. In this hierar-
chical society grounded in practices of patron-
age and reciprocity, children offered nothing of
value. So of course the disciples tried to drive
off these annoying little "nobodies." Jesus was
far too important to spend his time with them.
When Jesus saw what the disciples were doing,
"he was indignant." Mark's use of the word
indignant reveals the depth of Jesus' emotions
on this matter. In rejecting these children, his
disciples had missed the whole point of his ministry. Taking the children in his arms, Jesus tells
the disciples, "It is to such as these that the kingdom of God belongs. Truly I tell you, whoever
does not receive the kingdom of God as a little
child will never enter it" (10:15). Jesus was not
sentimentalizing little children. He was, however, proclaiming that the home we are invited
to live in, this kingdom of God, is intended
for the least powerful and the most vulnerable.
That includes children, or refugees, or people
on welfare, or undocumented workers. And
that includes you and me when we are made
vulnerable by life's hardships or brought low by
our own darkness. Jesus tells us that we have a

home in God's realm of compassion, love, and acceptance.

HOMEWARD BOUND

How do we find this home? Where is this kingdom of God? One of the religious leaders comes to Jesus and asks him which of the commandments is the greatest. Jesus answers with what were two familiar commandments: "Hear, O Israel: the Lord our God, the Lord is one; you shall love the Lord your God with all your heart, and with all your soul, and with all your mind, and with all your strength," and "You shall love your neighbor as yourself" (12:29–31). The religious leader affirms Jesus' answer, and he adds that these two commandments are more important than any of the elaborate religious rituals people carry out at the temple, where he himself makes a living. When Jesus hears how well this man answers, Jesus says to him, "You are not far from the kingdom of God" (v. 34). Not far! This leader's words offer a clue about where we can find the kingdom of God. We find our way into the kingdom of God when we accept God's love for us and then when we turn around and follow Jesus on the path of loving God and our neighbors—*all* of our neighbors. *That's* the path home.

God offers us the privilege of extending home to one another. Offering people home is more than just being friendly and nice. It involves reaching out to include others, working for justice for those denied a sense of home, creating opportunities for people to rebuild their lives after mistakes or hardships, surrounding those brought low with support and care.

The church I serve, located right next to a large university, attracts a fair number of students to our services. Some years ago, a Chinese graduate student began to worship with us. He was not a Christian, but freed from the oversight of his government he was curious to learn about Christianity first-hand. He seemed eager to spend time with us. I recall one Sunday when he made church an all-day affair by attending both of our morning services, the adult class in between the services, and the potluck afterward! In talking with him we learned that he had left his wife and two small children back in China in order to study in the United States. Members of the church started inviting him to other church events and to their homes and offered assistance with some of his basic needs. The student had been attending for about a month when he shared with me, "The first three months I was in this country I was very lonely. But then after coming to this church, I feel as if I have found a family." Those were the best words a pastor or her congregation could hope to hear. Before he returned to China, he shared with me that he found it meaningful to read the Bible every day.

In C. S. Lewis's famous novel *The Lion, the Witch, and the Wardrobe*, four siblings discover that they can enter a completely new world by walking through the back of an old wardrobe. When they push past the garments hanging in this ordinary household piece of furniture, they discover a portal to the fantastical world of Narnia.

Imagine that there are portals all around us, every day, that lead to this new realm called the kingdom of God. Whenever we seize the opportunities that arise in our ordinary lives to love God and love our neighbor, we will have stepped through the portal and into the kingdom of God. These portals are found everywhere, if we only look. You go to school—there's a portal. You go to work—there's a portal. You are standing in line at the grocery store—there's a portal. A neighbor's spouse dies—there's a portal. You are disturbed by what a new government policy will do to low-income families—there's a portal. The kingdom of God is a parallel universe, and all around us are portals to this other domain. We just have to see them and walk through, which we do any time we offer grace, forgiveness, compassion, generosity, justice, and acceptance, and any time we accept God's healing, transforming love for ourselves. And when we do, we will be transported to our true home.

At the end of *The Wizard of Oz*, Dorothy discovers that the ruby red slippers on her feet are in fact a portal for her to return home. All she has to do is click her heels together three times and say, "There's no place like home," and she will be transported home again. It turns out that throughout her odyssey she had the means to go home with her the entire time. And so do we. We have the means to go home right with us.

Some may recall a famous television episode where talk show host Oprah Winfrey gave away a new car to every member of the audience, pointing her finger and shouting out to the screaming crowd, "*You* get a car! And *you* get a car! *Everyone* gets a car!"[5] In the gift-giving Christmas season, we celebrate the most precious gift of all—the home of love and acceptance God offers to each of us, and the well-being of body and soul we can offer one another. The season invites us to imagine Jesus Christ beckoning us to enter the kingdom of God, proclaiming with love, "*You* get a home! And *you* get a home! *Everyone* gets a home!"

Questions for Contemplation or Discussion

1. How has your personal history of home influenced how you feel about Christmas?
2. Where in the world or in your community has one group's quest for home (either physical or emotional) led to social or political conflict or even violence?

3. How does the notion of extended kinship and radical inclusion enhance or threaten your understanding of family?

4. Thinking of your patterns of thought and daily actions, where do you identify portals into the kingdom of God?

5. How might Jesus' teachings about the kingdom of God and radical inclusion affect the way you celebrate Christmas?

Chapter 4

HIDDEN IN PLAIN SIGHT

Secrets and Revelations of the Messiah

Jesus departed with his disciples to the lake, and a great multitude from Galilee followed him; hearing all that he was doing, they came to him in great numbers from Judea, Jerusalem, Idumea, beyond the Jordan, and the region around Tyre and Sidon. He told his disciples to have a boat ready for him because of the crowd, so that they would not crush him; for he had cured many, so that all who had diseases pressed upon him to touch him. Whenever the unclean spirits saw him, they fell down before him and shouted, "You are the Son of God!" But he sternly ordered them not to make him known. (Mark 3:7–12)

Jesus went on with his disciples to the villages of Caesarea Philippi; and on the way he asked his disciples, "Who do people say that I am?" And they answered him, "John the Baptist; and others, Elijah; and still others, one of the prophets." He asked them, "But who do you say that I am?" Peter answered him, "You are the Messiah." And he sternly ordered them not to tell anyone about him. (Mark 8:27–30)

Six days later, Jesus took with him Peter and James and John, and led them up a high mountain apart, by themselves. And he was transfigured before them, and his clothes became dazzling white, such as no one on earth could bleach them. And there appeared to them Elijah with Moses, who were talking with Jesus. Then Peter said to Jesus, "Rabbi, it is good for us to be here; let us make three dwellings, one for you, one for Moses, and one for Elijah." He did not know what to say, for they were terrified. Then a cloud overshadowed them, and from the cloud there came a voice, "This is my Son, the Beloved; listen to him!" Suddenly when they looked around, they saw no one with them any more, but only Jesus.

As they were coming down the mountain, he ordered them to tell no one about what they had seen, until after the Son of Man had risen from the dead. So they kept the matter to themselves, questioning what this rising from the dead could mean. (Mark 9:2–10)

MY TWO YOUNG CHILDREN AND I WERE standing in line to get lunch at a sandwich shop when I saw my five-year-old son eyeing the pastry display case. Looking up at me he stated, "We should have a welcome home party for Dad tonight." My husband had been traveling but was due home that evening. I was pretty sure where this conversation was headed. I replied, "Well, that's a nice idea. You mean just the four of us?" I asked. "Yes," my son responded. "And we could buy one of those cakes for the party," he added pointing to the display case. Despite the self-interest that I was confident had inspired my son's sudden burst of thoughtfulness, I agreed and bought the cake. That evening as I placed the cake on the dining room table and laid out some paper party napkins left over from a previous event, my three-year-old daughter followed behind me, watching wide-eyed but silent. Now the festive table was all ready as a surprise when we came home from the airport with their dad. But as we pulled into the driveway with my husband, my daughter suddenly remembered what lay waiting for us inside the house. "Party on the table, Dad! Party on the table!" she exclaimed in her high voice. Confused by what she was saying, my husband asked her what she meant, but my daughter just kept repeating, "Party on the table!" My son, desperate to salvage the surprise, jumped into the conversation. "No! There's no party on the table, and there's no cake either!" It was some time before I could stop laughing and help my husband make sense of what had just taken place.

There is a time for secrets, and there is a time for revelation. Christmas is the season for both. We conspire in hushed whispers with one or two members of our household about what gifts to get the other people in our house. Then, after procuring the gifts in secret, we hide them away in some dark corner of the house until we can conceal them beneath beautiful wrapping paper and lay them under the tree. Then we wait for the "big reveal"—Christmas Eve or Christmas morning when our loved ones will tear off the wrappings and disclose the hidden contents. We watch our loved ones' reactions with nervous anticipation to see if this revelation brings them joy or disappointment. The best Christmas morning gift disclosure in our house was when our children were quite young and my husband and I gave them a hamster. When they lifted the gift-wrapped box off the cage and saw the furry little creature, they were completely surprised and totally elated, and they ran circles around the room in utter joy. As parents, it was our most satisfying Christmas morning revelation.

The Gospel writers of Matthew and Luke also give us very satisfying Christmas revelations in their stories of Jesus' birth. In fact, these stories are so pleasing to us that people of faith have reenacted them down through the centuries in annual church pageants and dramas. In Luke we learn about the heavenly band of angels that appears to the shepherds and announces the birth of the Messiah, telling them where the child can be found. The shepherds go and see this revelation for themselves. We are told that "the shepherds returned, glorifying and praising God for all they had heard and seen" (Luke 2:20). In Matthew's Gospel we read about the bright star in the sky that reveals to the wise men where the newborn king of the Jews can be found. The role of the magi in the story symbolizes the revealing of the good news of the Messiah's birth to the gentile world. The secret is getting out; it is being told beyond the Jewish world. The wise men follow this star and finally come to the place where the child is found. Scripture tells us that the magi "were overwhelmed with joy" upon finding the child (Matt. 2:10).

Matthew's and Luke's Gospels offer us these "Ta-da! Here is the Messiah!" kind of moments, these grand revelations of great joy about Jesus. In Mark's Gospel, however, the revelation of the Messiah is generally not so straightforward. There are occasions in Mark's Gospel where Jesus' identity as the Messiah is openly revealed—in the first sentence, for example, where Mark writes, "The beginning of the good news of Jesus Christ, the Son of God" (1:1). Yet frequently throughout the Gospel, Mark portrays a Messiah who attempts to conceal his identity. Even as he goes about healing and driving out demons from people, performing miraculous actions like feeding the multitudes and calming the stormy sea, Jesus is also trying to keep his identity a secret. He constantly tells people who know who he is to hush up. When the unclean spirits correctly identify Jesus as "the Son of God," Jesus orders them to be quiet (3:7–12). When he heals a leper and a deaf man and raises a little girl from the dead, he instructs them all to tell no one what he has done (1:40–43; 7:32–36; 5:35–43). When Jesus asks his disciples who they think he is and Peter says, "You are the Messiah," Jesus warns them to tell no one (8:27–30). This odd "messianic secret" has puzzled scholars and people of faith through the ages. Why would Jesus conceal his identity?

Some secrets are meant to be shared, but only at the right time. Our gift-giving secrets, for example, are hidden from our loved ones only temporarily, with the ultimate intention of their being revealed on Christmas morning. There is evidence that Mark's Jesus intended his secret to be disclosed but only at the right moment. Jesus took time to explain a challenging parable to his disciples, stating, "For there is nothing hidden, except to be disclosed; nor is anything secret, except to come to light" (4:22). It seems likely that Jesus kept his identity secret from all but a few people because it was not yet the right time to share it. When Jesus had that amazing moment up on the mountain when he was transfigured before his disciples and God's voice declared, "This is my Son, the Beloved," Jesus later told Peter, James, and John to "tell no one about what they had seen, *until after* the Son of Man had risen from the dead" (9:9; emphasis added). There would come a time when that revelation would need to be shared—but not yet.

"Why not?" we may ask. It is likely that a premature revelation of the Messiah could have led a misguided group of people to fashion Jesus into a Messiah of their own creation. People might have jumped to the wrong conclusion and embraced a misunderstanding of who this "king" and "messiah" would be—one who would help them drive out the Romans and restore Israel to greatness. Thus, Jesus needed to keep his identity concealed to the outside world.

KINGDOM CLUES

Despite the secret, Jesus certainly gave profound hints about his identity. In some curious and puzzling parables, Jesus illustrates the alternative nature of the kingdom of God and its Messiah. In one parable, Jesus states that the kingdom of God is like someone who scatters seeds on the ground that then grow and bear fruit in unseen and mysterious ways (4:26–29). God's kingdom and the work of its Messiah would come to fruition but in hidden ways, not in noticeable demonstrations of power and might.

Jesus offers a second parable, stating that the kingdom of God is like a mustard seed, which is the smallest of seeds and yet when sown grows to become a great bush in which the birds of the air can nest in its branches (4:30–32). Those listening to this parable would have understood

that Jesus was making a joke. Mustard plants
were invasive weeds, not something anyone
would ever intentionally plant. And listeners
would have also understood the allusion Jesus
was making to a passage in Ezekiel about the
mighty cedar tree, which served as an allegory
for the restoration of the Davidic kingdom. In
the Ezekiel passage, God plants a noble cedar
tree on a high mountain, and in its branches
birds of the air make their nests. God declares,
"I bring low the high tree and make high the
low tree" (Ezekiel 17:24). Jesus takes the Ezekiel passage and turns it on its head. Instead of
a noble cedar tree as a symbol of God's activity, Jesus gives us a lowly mustard bush! Buried
in this odd parable is an astonishing proposi-
tion. Could the much-anticipated reign of God
really come about through a Messiah born in
poverty to people of no account, or through the
socially marginalized people he reached out to
in love? Jesus alludes to God's kingdom, and
by extension himself, as a hidden, mysterious
presence that, like an invasive weed, lies beyond
our ability to control or manage, a realm in

which the lowly are raised up and the powerful brought low.

Jesus shared these cryptic stories about the realm of God with the crowds, but in private, among his small group of disciples, he offered words of explanation. And it is to this small group of followers that Jesus also gradually disclosed his identity. Three times Jesus shared with his followers that the Messiah would be handed over to enemies, killed, and would rise again after three days (8:31; 9:31; 10:32–34). The disciples failed to understand, and in fact, as with Peter's rebuke of Jesus, actively resisted this concept of the Messiah (8:32). Jesus again revealed the truth about the Messiah when he told his disciples, "Whoever wishes to be first among you must be slave of all. For the Son of Man came not to be served but to serve, and to give his life a ransom for many" (10:44–45).

Jesus not only *told* his disciples who he was, but he publicly *demonstrated* his identity through his miracles and acts of compassion. Jesus manifested himself for all to see by the way he healed the sick, cared about the vulnerable, and confronted dark and oppressive forces. Yet many people, including the disciples on most occasions, failed to grasp his identity. In two separate stories, Jesus heals a blind person (8:22; 10:46), yet both healing accounts are framed by stories of the disciples remaining persistently "blind" about the nature of Jesus and his realm, raising the question among us readers about just who is truly blind. An incredulous Jesus even asks his disciples at one point, "Do you have eyes, and fail to see?" (8:18).

Over and over again, Jesus reveals himself through his acts of compassion and love. Some of the people perceive who he is. Many do not. The Messiah is hidden in plain sight, visible to those who have the spiritual insight to discern the presence of God revealed through this man but hidden from those who expect the Messiah to come in another form.

In the song *Carol of the Epiphany*, John Bell writes about the magi's search for Christ. The first three verses are sung from the perspective of each of the magi and their surprise at where Christ is discovered. The magi join their voices together in the fourth and fifth verses.

I sought him dressed in finest clothes, where
    money talks and status grows;
but power and wealth he never chose: It
    seemed he lived in poverty.

I sought him in the safest place, remote from
    crime or cheap disgrace;
but safety never knew his face: It seemed he
    lived in jeopardy.

I sought him where the spotlights glare,
    where crowds collect and critics stare;
but no one knew his presence there: It
    seemed he lived in obscurity.

Then, in the streets, we heard the word that
    seemed, for all the world, absurd:
That those who could no gifts afford were
    entertaining Christ the Lord.

And so, distinct from all we'd planned,
    among the poorest of the land,
we did what few might understand: We
    touched God in a baby's hand.[1]

The song beckons us to join the magi in search-
ing for the Messiah, and it invites us to consider

that Christ is likely to be revealed among those who live, as the song suggests, in poverty, jeopardy, and obscurity.

DISCOVERING JESUS

Outside the parking lot entrance to the church I serve is a receptacle for smokers to deposit their cigarettes so they won't litter the church property with their discarded butts. However, there are some individuals in the neighborhood who, when walking through our lot, will pull the insert out of the receptacle and dump the contents on the ground in order to search for used cigarette butts they can finish smoking. When they do this, it leaves a big mess of ash and cigarette butts everywhere—the very mess we were trying to avoid by having the receptacle in the first place. One day I drove into the church parking lot just in time to witness a woman dumping the insert on the ground and begin picking through the butts. Aha! I had caught one of the culprits in the act. I jumped out of my car and marched over to the woman. "I hope you are going to pick up every one of those butts!" I barked at her. She jumped up, clearly startled. And then she began yelling, "You get away from me, you woman!" She turned and fled across the parking lot, still yelling at me. As I turned to leave, I thought to myself, "I probably could have handled that better." And thinking more about the encounter, I thought, "I *really* could have handled that better." I thought about how the woman must have felt having me just run up and bark at her that way, and how many other people she likely encountered in her daily rounds who made her feel unwelcome. And I thought about the life circumstances that would lead this woman to look for used cigarette butts to smoke. I thought about my role models of faith, those people who help me see the way of Jesus and how they would have handled that situation. And I thought about Jesus. Not only did I not recognize Jesus in her, but I did not do what Jesus would have done.

It takes practice to see Jesus. And it takes a community of others to help us see Jesus. Because sometimes Jesus, hidden in plain sight, looks more like a mustard bush than a cedar tree.

Yet even when we do discover Jesus, we sometimes don't like the implications of this revelation. Peter did not like Jesus' revelation that the Messiah would suffer and be rejected and be killed. That did not match the image he had of a messiah who would forcefully assume command, demand respect, and exert his will on his enemies. So Peter tried to shut down that conversation. He took Jesus aside and told him to stop talking like that (8:31–33).

In a similar way, our encounters with Jesus, his revelation of our shortcomings, and his expectations of us can make us uncomfortable and resistant to the truth. We don't like facing the racism that is embedded in our institutions and internalized in our minds and hearts, or the reality of climate change, or our personal problems with drinking or spending or anger. Like Peter, we may try to shut down such uncomfortable conversations. Yet issues such as these are "hidden in plain sight," operating quite openly, causing enduring harm to God's children. Christ is revealed in us when we find the courage to confront the hidden and harmful parts of ourselves and our society and seek God's transformational power.

In a favorite Christmas hymn, "O Little Town of Bethlehem," we beseech Christ to "be born in us today." Christ comes into our lives so that his way and his love might be born in us, revealed in us. What would someone learn about us by looking at our checkbooks or credit card statements, by examining our appointment calendars, or by stepping into our homes? What about the way of Christ would be revealed? Or do our choices, lifestyles, and priorities obscure Christ from being known to others or even to ourselves?

Perhaps it would seem a lot easier to follow Jesus and his way if he were as apparent as the billboards we pass on our highways. Yet it is also possible that Christ's concealment actually enriches our faith. Sometimes the insights that have the most lasting impact upon us are those we discover for ourselves. My husband teaches college students and has the opportunity to instruct students in two distinct ways. One method of learning, the classic form of education, takes place with the students sitting in a classroom while he lectures to them. The other form of learning occurs when students accompany him on academic seminars to places around the globe where they experience the subject matters firsthand. You can no doubt imagine which form of learning has the greatest impact. Perhaps the hidden nature of Christ functions in a similar way—inviting us on a personal journey of discovering the presence of the Messiah for ourselves. Much the way a good mystery novel engages the reader in the journey to solve the case, Christ's concealment, hidden yet still accessible, draws us into deeper engagement as we seek to discover where Christ will be revealed in our lives.

Then too, perhaps the writer of Mark's Gospel offers only gradual glimpses of revelation as a safeguard against human arrogance. Revelation without any appreciation for the mystery of God becomes certitude. As witnessed throughout human history, certitude in any religious tradition easily leads to intolerance toward others. In addition, certitude becomes idolatrous toward God. To know with certainty is to possess, to control, and to manage. And God will not be possessed, controlled, or managed. Unlike mystery, certitude silences curiosity. It implies that you've got God all figured out. Yet mystery invites curiosity and encourages us to puzzle, to explore, and to discover what eludes us. Thus, the mystery of the Messiah and his kingdom beckons the disciples and us readers into a journey of discovery.

Even though the messianic secret appears throughout Mark's Gospel, there are in fact three very clear moments when the writer reveals Jesus' identity. At Jesus' baptism, the heavens are "torn apart," the Spirit descends, and God's voice declares, "You are my Son, the Beloved" (1:10–11). Later, in the middle of his ministry, Jesus goes up the mountain and has that experience we call "the transfiguration," when his clothes become dazzling white and God's voice again declares, "This is my Son, the Beloved" (9:7).

Yet for Mark, the most significant moment of revelation comes at the very end—at the crucifixion. The crucifixion is Mark's big "Ta-da! Here is the Messiah!" revelation. Mark's whole Gospel account has been building to this climatic moment when we are shown a suffering, vulnerable Messiah hanging on a cross between two bandits.

Not only does Mark not have a birth story, but many people feel that Mark lacks a satisfactory version of the resurrection. In the traditional ending to Mark, the women come to the tomb but do not find the risen Christ. Instead, they are met by an angelic figure who tells them, "He has been raised; he is not here. . . . But go, tell his disciples and Peter that he is going ahead of you to Galilee; there you will see him" (16:6–7). The women run away in fear. And that's where the traditional version of Mark's Gospel ends, without any sighting of the risen Jesus. It appears as though the risen Christ is hidden from our sight. Yet the angel beckons us to seek Christ beyond the tomb—there we will see him. Mark ends the Gospel with this same revelation/concealment paradox. Christ is risen, but it remains for you and me to discover his presence in all the places and circumstances where he goes ahead of us.

Questions for Contemplation or Discussion

1. Jesus, as he is portrayed by Mark, inverted expectations about a coming Messiah. What were those expectations, and how was Jesus so radically different? How does the parable about the mustard seed and its comparison to the cedar tree alluded to by the prophet Ezekiel illustrate this inversion?

2. People sometimes feel that God is "revealed" or known in times of joy, success, or prosperity and is absent in times of hardship. What does this perspective disclose about our understanding of God? What does this mindset reveal about how we may regard those who suffer, who are vulnerable, or who are economically disadvantaged?

3. If Jesus is not the "macho" Messiah so many people expected, what sort of Messiah was he? What difference does this make for your faith?

4. What does it say to you that Mark leaves out both a nativity story and a robust resurrection story?

5. In what ways might Mark's version of Jesus be born in you this Christmas season?

Chapter 5

THE CRADLE, THE CROSS, AND THE GIFT OF EMMANUEL

Now the birth of Jesus the Messiah took place in this way. When his mother Mary had been engaged to Joseph, but before they lived together, she was found to be with child from the Holy Spirit. Her husband Joseph, being a righteous man and unwilling to expose her to public disgrace, planned to dismiss her quietly. But just when he had resolved to do this, an angel of the Lord appeared to him in a dream and said, "Joseph, son of David, do not be afraid to take Mary as your wife, for the child conceived in her is from the Holy Spirit. She will bear a son, and you are to name him Jesus, for he will save his people from their sins." All this took place to fulfill what had been spoken by the Lord through the prophet:

> "Look, the virgin shall conceive and bear a son,
>   and they shall name him Emmanuel,"

which means, "God is with us."

(Matt. 1:18–23)

When it was noon, darkness came over the whole land until three in the afternoon. At three o'clock Jesus cried out with a loud voice, "Eloi, Eloi, lema sabachthani?" which means, "My God, my God, why have you forsaken me?" When some of the bystanders heard it, they said, "Listen, he is calling for Elijah." And someone ran, filled a sponge with sour wine, put it on a stick, and gave it to him to drink, saying, "Wait, let us see whether Elijah will come to take him down." Then Jesus gave a loud cry and breathed his last. And the curtain of the temple was torn in two, from top to bottom. Now when the centurion, who stood facing him, saw that in this way he breathed his last, he said, "Truly this man was God's Son!" (Mark 15:33–39)

THE PAGEANT AND WORSHIP SERVICE CAME to an end. As the congregation was milling about, with worshipers wishing one another "Merry Christmas," I noticed something odd taking place on the stage. The children in the pageant had not moved but remained kneeling in their places. This was the family Christmas Eve service in which the children reenacted the nativity story in a costumed pageant. Aside from a few key actors selected in advance, any child who attended the service could join in the pageant on the spot and was swiftly outfitted in head coverings, tunics, and halos, depending upon his or her choice of character. A baby doll stood in for the infant Jesus. The drama concluded with all the characters kneeling around Mary as she held the baby and the congregation singing "Away in a Manger." The service was now over, so why hadn't the children gotten up? I noticed that many of the children had crowded closer around Mary and were leaning over to get a better look at the baby Jesus. One of the children said something, and then Mary passed him the baby. The little boy gently held the doll, gazing down upon it, when the girl next to him nudged him, and he then handed the baby over to her. The doll continued to get passed around in this fashion to the cluster of kneeling children, each eager to get his or her time with the baby. It was nothing more than a doll—and yet somehow in the enactment of the story the doll had been transformed into someone who inspired awe, reverence, and a sense of mystery in these children.

Such is the power that the nativity story has on many of us. Christmas brings us all metaphorically to the cradle to gaze upon the infant Jesus with awe and reverence. While the sight of any newborn baby is likely to inspire feelings of tenderness, the birth of Jesus stirs within us deeper emotions of wonder and mystery. This is no ordinary baby; it is somehow also the very presence of the Divine. In John's Gospel we are told, "The Word was with God, and the Word was God. . . . And the Word became flesh and lived among us" (John 1:1, 14). In Matthew's Gospel the angel of the Lord refers to Mary's yet unborn child as "Emmanuel," which means "God with us" (Matt. 1:23).

The incarnation is the essence of the Christmas story—that God took on human flesh and entered our lives in the person of Jesus. God became human. On Christmas we gather around Jesus' cradle and gaze with awe at how God came to us as, of all things, a baby! It is revealing that instead of coming into our lives in a superhero's suit, ready to take on the evil of this world with power and might, God brought hope to us by entering this world as all of us do—as a vulnerable, helpless baby. The beauty of Christmas lies in the surprising fact that God would choose to enter our human condition and affirm our worth.

The Gospel of Mark, however, offers us a different perspective on the incarnation. Without a birth narrative, we won't find Mark's interpretation of the incarnation by looking for the babe in the manger. If the incarnation were to end at the Christmas story it would be a vastly incomplete account, for humans are not only born but grow up, know joys and struggles, and eventually die. For Mark, the incarnation is revealed in the God who walks with us through the triumphs and tragedies of life and ultimately to our deaths. That is why the incarnational events in Mark are found not in the sweet baby Jesus in the cradle but in Jesus' life and ministry and especially in Jesus' dying on the cross. Throughout Mark's Gospel, Emmanuel is revealed in the one who was baptized in the Jordan and tempted in the wilderness, who fed the hungry and touched the outcasts with compassion, who healed the sick and calmed the seas, who confronted the powerful and noticed the powerless, who sat around a table and shared meals with his disciples. While Jesus often tried to conceal his identity from the public, those with spiritual insight could ascertain a holy presence in the man who joined them in these extraordinary activities. God was with them.

Much like a snowball rolling down hill, Mark's disclosure of Jesus as Emmanuel gains momentum through the course of the Gospel as it heads toward the crucifixion. In three distinct accounts in Mark's Gospel, Jesus is proclaimed to be the Son of God. The title "Son of God" conveyed multiple meanings in those ancient times, but it was often used as a royal title for kings (e.g., 2 Samuel 7:14). However, it is clear from Mark's Gospel that it implied a status for Jesus that went well beyond an earthly kingship. At Jesus' baptism we read that the heavenly barrier separating God from this world was torn apart, revealing that the one who stood dripping wet there in the Jordan River was somehow God's very presence. And God declared, "You are my Son, the Beloved" (1:11). Again, up on the mountain of transfiguration, Jesus stood in the company of Moses and Elijah. But Jesus was the only one of the three bathed in God's glory. It was only for Jesus whom God declared, "This is my Son, the Beloved; listen to him!" (9:9). Listening to Jesus is equated with listening to God.

The final declaration of Jesus as Son of God occurs at the crucifixion. Ironically, this revelation of God's presence in the dying Christ was first declared by the Roman centurion presiding at Jesus' execution. Whether or not this soldier understood the true meaning of his words, it was he who declared upon witnessing Jesus' death, "Truly this man was God's Son!" (15:39). While Mark maintains the distinctiveness of the

Creator and the Son, he also emphasizes their inseparability. It is clear that Mark believes that Jesus enjoys some share of the divine presence.

Mark's description of the crucifixion itself further underscores the presence of God in the one suffering upon the cross. Mark writes that when Jesus died, the curtain of the temple was "torn in two" (15:38). This curtain separated the Holy of Holies, where God was believed to dwell, from the rest of the temple in order to protect the priests from accidentally gazing upon God's face and perishing. No one could enter the Holy of Holies except for the high priest, and then only once a year with his head bowed down. When Jesus takes his last breath, this thick curtain is ripped in half, and the once-hidden God is made accessible, not just to temple leadership but to all people. There on the cross, in the figure of the suffering and dying Jesus, Emmanuel is seen and known.

For Mark, the decisive revelation of Emmanuel, of Jesus being "God with us," comes at the crucifixion. At the cross, Jesus' ultimate accompaniment with humanity is unveiled for all to see. God wasn't just born in flesh or living in a human body; God came to the final end that all human beings experience: death. The death of the Son of God becomes the definitive sign of God enfleshed as a human being. Matthew's cradle is Mark's cross.

GOD JOINS US

Mark doesn't give us a thoroughly developed theology of the cross—why Jesus had to die, or what Jesus' death means for us. That would be the work of theologians—the apostle Paul, the writer of John's Gospel, and others—down through the centuries. Rather, Mark takes us by the hand, leads us to the cross, and points, saying, "There. There is God." And from that event, people found hope.

Now how can there be any hope in *that*—in suffering and in death? Some people are turned off by Christianity's focus on the cross, arguing that Christians revel in violence and suffering. Think for example of medieval crucifixes where the bloodied Christ is on full display or Christian hymns that focus on the blood of Jesus that washes "white as snow." Others regard the cross as symbolic of all that is wretched about the human condition—our propensity for violence and hatred and brutality—and thus it could never offer any measure of hope. Christians themselves have, throughout the centuries, wrestled to understand the cross. Some Christians interpret the crucifixion as the means by which a wrathful God's anger is satisfied—an interpretation that for many people does not inspire feelings of trust or affection toward their Creator.

Theologian Douglas John Hall writes that the cross reveals "not that God thinks humankind so wretched that it deserves death and hell, but that God thinks humankind and the whole creation so good, so beautiful, so precious in its intention and its potentiality, that its actualization, its fulfillment, its redemption is worth dying for."[1] The cross is not a sign of God's cruel desire to inflict pain and suffering. Rather, pain and suffering exist in this world, and God loves this world. So God enters the pain of this world. Hall maintains that God is always moving toward this world in love. He writes, "The crucifixion, which is no glorious thing, as event, is nonetheless celebratory as symbol; that is, in our Good Friday remembrance of it, Christians celebrate the victorious decision of the Christ to traverse this final sad portion of the Via Dolorosa, to take this final step toward the world God loves."[2]

Yes, the cross does indeed reveal humanity's wretchedness. Every day our world is full of endless accounts of human cruelty and suffering: of desperate refugees dying on the seas, of women being exploited and children being abused, of starvation and torture and warfare. But instead of abandoning us to this grim reality, God *enters* this reality. The incarnation is not only about God coming to stand in solidarity with us, joining us in the darkness of our pain and brokenness, but also going with us to the tomb.

Sarah Klassen's poem "Incarnation" speaks to the meaning found in a God who is with us:

God is carnal? Yes! God
has got to be flesh and blood. Bones too
like any one of us. A child
can't go to sleep in a dark room

unless someone is right there beside her.
Someone with some skin.[3]

Someone with some skin. The incarnation is about God who comes to us in the flesh, with skin and bones and blood, who enters the dark rooms of our lives, our souls, and our world. We are not alone in the dark. God is with us.

The incarnation reminds us that God's love for us is never abstract. Love is only meaningful when it takes a tangible form, when it becomes enfleshed. God didn't stand at a distance and simply *tell* us we are loved. Instead, God came to us in the flesh, as Jesus, because God knows that the darkness can be frightening even to adults. We need the tangible embodiment of God's love and mercy to heal us, comfort us, and bring us hope.

But where is this incarnate Christ now? In our present era, two thousand years after Jesus lived, where are we to find the embodied Jesus?

THE HOUR GREW late when Jesus was teaching a crowd of five thousand, so the disciples suggested that Jesus send the crowds to the nearby towns to find something to eat. Jesus turned to his followers and said, "You give them something to eat." When Jesus' disciples were flabbergasted at the impossibility of the task in front of them, Jesus showed them how it is done. And a miracle took place (Mark 6:30–44).

You do it! That's Christ's message to us, his followers. *You* feed the hungry. *You* share what you have. *You* care for the poor. *You* give second chances. *You* stand up for the powerless. *You* comfort the grieving. Christ summons us to be his presence in the world so that others may know Emmanuel, that God is with them. Love becomes embodied on those nights when you are up late with a feverish child, feeding her ice chips or putting a cold cloth on his head. Love is made tangible as you chop vegetables to make soup for your ill neighbor. Love takes form when you stock the shelves at a food pantry in your community or as you write a letter to your member of Congress about a social issue.

Indeed, that is what Christians are called to be for the world—the tangible embodiment of Christ's presence. In fact, the apostle Paul described the Christian community as "the body of Christ." The church becomes the hands, the feet, the heart, the skin, the presence of Christ in the world.

In order to embody Christ, we must, like him, be willing to walk with him into the world's darkness and pain. Jesus tells the crowds, "If any want to become my followers, let them deny themselves and take up their cross and follow me" (8:34). Once again we confront the cross, only this time it's our own! Loving this world with Christ's disruptive love involves effort, sacrifice, and a readiness to experience opposition. Mark's Jesus makes it clear that there is indeed a cost to discipleship, and the cross symbolizes that cost. This cost is not rooted in wrath or vengeance toward us or others but is grounded in God's love, justice, and mercy.

GOOD FRIDAY TRANSFORMED

It is especially tragic when instead of serving as the body of Christ, the Christian church embodies the darkness and brokenness of this world. During the period between 1880 and 1940, approximately five thousand African Americans were lynched in the United States. Sometimes these crimes were publicized in advance in local papers and conducted as public spectacles with as many as twenty thousand men, women, and children attending. Postcards were sometimes made of the white lynchers and spectators standing in front of the hanging bodies.

Theologian James Cone draws a parallel between the lynching of blacks in the United States and the crucifixion of Jesus. "Theologically speaking," Cone writes, "Jesus was the 'first lynchee,' who foreshadowed all the lynched black bodies on American soil. He was crucified by the same principalities and powers that lynched black people in America."[4] How especially distressing it is to realize that most often the people conducting these atrocities could be found singing hymns on Sunday morning in the pews of their neighborhood churches.

In the two thousand years since Jesus' crucifixion, history has revealed with disturbing frequency the failure of Christians to embody his love and grace. Whether through their intolerance and exclusion of one another or through their conquest of peoples and lands, Christians have perpetrated, sanctioned, or permitted great suffering of other human beings—the people whom the Salvadoran martyr Ignacio Ellacuria called "the crucified peoples of history."

What is to become of us when even the followers of Christ fail so profoundly? The only hope we have lies in what we celebrate at Christmas: the incarnation. Into our darkness comes God, in the flesh. Jesus entered our world to lead us from darkness to light. Rather than rejecting us for all our failures, God draws close to us in love. The incarnation is the story of God's fierce love for humanity and steadfast solidarity with us in our darkness in order that God might transform that darkness. That transformative love is found on the cross and then is further revealed in the empty tomb—at the resurrection.

Mark's account of the Easter story is so brief one might conclude the writer had little interest in the resurrection. But a closer look at the entire Gospel reveals Mark's profound focus on the resurrection. In the very first chapter, Jesus enters Simon Peter's house and is told that Peter's mother-in-law is in bed with a fever. This was probably more than just a bad head cold but something fairly serious, an illness that could possibly mean her death. Her illness would have also rendered her "unclean" and cut her off from her larger community. Mark explains that Jesus took her by the hand and "lifted her up." This phrase, translated in the New Revised Standard Version as "lifted her up," in the original Greek literally means "raised up." The word *egeiro* is the same word used at the end of Mark's Gospel when the angel in the tomb tells the women that Jesus "has been raised up; he is not here." In other words, the healing of Peter's mother-in-law is a resurrection. Healed of her potentially fatal illness and restored to full inclusion in her community, the mother-in-law is raised to new life. This is a story of a cross and a resurrection.

But there's more! In chapter 2, people bring a paralyzed man to Jesus for healing. As a disabled person, he too would have been shunned as "unclean." Jesus says to this man, "Stand up, take your mat and go to your home," again using that same Greek word, *egeiro* (v. 11). Another cross and another resurrection.

In the next chapter, Jesus encounters a man with a withered hand. It's the Sabbath day, when no work is supposed to take place, so the religious leaders are watching Jesus to see if he will violate the rules. Jesus does not disappoint them. Jesus calls the man to him, saying, "Come forward" (*egeiro*). And he heals the man. Again, someone's cross-bearing experience is succeeded by a resurrection.

In chapter 5 the father of a little girl who has fallen terribly ill begs Jesus to heal her. But by the time Jesus gets to the home, the family announces that she has already perished. Nevertheless, Jesus goes into her room, takes her by the hand, and says, "Little girl, get up!" (v. 41). Want to guess what Greek word Jesus uses? *Egeiro!* Another cross followed by another resurrection.

In chapter 9 it's a boy who suffers from epilepsy. When the boy's father seeks healing for his child, the boy has a seizure right in front of Jesus. Jesus takes him by the hand and lifts him up. Our favorite Greek word appears again—*egeiro.* The boy is healed and given new life. Another cross is replaced with a resurrection.

It turns out that the Gospel of Mark is chock-full of resurrections! We thought resurrection was something that happened *to* Jesus.

But as it turns out, Jesus' life was a ministry of resurrection. Long before Jesus faced his own crucifixion and experienced his own resurrection, he was meeting people in their Good Friday moments of death and suffering and pain, becoming Emmanuel to them and raising them to new life. The resurrection does indeed include the promise of life beyond the grave—but it is also clear from Mark that God's resurrection power does not wait until we die. Christ raises us to new life while we yet live and breathe.

THE GIFT OF HOPE

At the age of fourteen, Christian Picciolini was radicalized by a group of neo-Nazis. By the age of sixteen he had risen in the white nationalist movement to become the leader of a skinhead group in Chicago. For years he preached a message of hate, carried out acts of violence, and convinced other people to join in acts of aggression. One day he and a group of his neo-Nazi followers chased an African American man out of a bar and proceeded to brutally beat him for no other reason than the color of his skin. As the man lay curled up on the ground, bloodied and swollen while the group kicked him, Christian recalls that the man opened his eyes and made eye contact with him. In that moment, Christian suddenly saw the man's humanity and for the first time had empathy for one of his victims. This awakening resulted in his distancing and ultimately severing all ties with the white nationalist movement. Where he once had promoted hate, Christian devoted himself to bringing healing, counseling other individuals trying to leave hate groups, and serving as a consultant for law enforcement.[5]

That moment when his victim looked Christian in the eye was an awakening, when Christian saw who he had become and was inspired to be something else. Perhaps we might think about Jesus on the cross as the occasion when Jesus looks *us* right in the eye, when Jesus connects with our darkness, our pain, our confusion, our feelings of being lost, our emptiness. Jesus looks us in the eye as we are caught up in our deep darkness and brokenness and says to us, "That's not all you have to be." There is more that God can do with each one of us. There is so much more potential in us than our brutality, and self-ishness, and pettiness, so much more than our frantic efforts to be successful and make money, so much more than our acquisition of stuff to fill our homes, so much more to us than the grudges we bear against one another, the bombs we drop, and the walls we build. The cross is a moment of brutality, for sure, but it is also a moment of awakening to the God who looks us in the eye with transforming love. We can be raised to new life. Our communities can be raised to new life.

The incarnation we celebrate at Christmas is the gift of hope given to you and to me. It is a hope grounded not in ourselves or our own goodness or our own potential, but rather in God's goodness and God's potential for us. Through God's transforming love, we can be people who offer kindness, and share our bread, and help refugees, and compose symphonies, and cure diseases, and offer forgiveness, and tear down walls between people. This is the gift of hope given to us in our darkness, given to our world in its darkness.

As we gather at the cradle, we find hope in

the new life God can birth in us. As we gaze at the cross, we see the way God enters the wretchedness of human existence with a love that transforms us. And we have hope.

Questions for Contemplation or Discussion

1. Normally when we think of Christmas, we think of Jesus in the manger and the gift of Christ to the world. Yet Mark's Gospel does not feature the birth of Jesus, focusing instead on the ministry, death, and resurrection of Jesus—themes we normally associate with Easter. How do you explain the connection between Easter and Christmas?

2. "Someone with some skin," wrote Sarah Klassen. The incarnation is about God who comes to us in the flesh, with skin and bones and blood, who enters the dark rooms of our lives, our souls, our world. In what way has the incarnation made a difference in your life? In what way *ought* the incarnation make a difference in the life of the Christian church?

3. Where have you recently seen tangible signs

of God's love? Where recently have you been privileged to embody Christ's love?

4. Douglas John Hall writes that "the crucifixion, which is no glorious thing, as event, is nonetheless celebratory as symbol." How do you respond to the idea of the crucifixion as something worth celebrating?

5. How has focusing on the life and death of Jesus during Advent changed your experience of Christmas this year?

DAILY SCRIPTURE
READING GUIDE

To immerse yourself even more deeply in the Gospel of Mark during Advent, follow this reading guide to work your way through the Gospel's sixteen chapters in just a few minutes per day.

Because Advent can vary in length from twenty-two days (if Christmas Day falls on a Monday) to twenty-eight days (if Christmas Day falls on a Sunday), this guide offers an undated twenty-four-day plan so you can either begin on December 1 and continue through Christmas Eve, or start on the First Sunday of Advent and adjust the schedule as you desire.

Day 1	1:1–28
Day 2	1:29–45
Day 3	2:1–28

Day 4	3:1–35
Day 5	4:1–34
Day 6	4:35–5:20
Day 7	5:21–43
Day 8	6:1–29
Day 9	6:30–56
Day 10	7:1–23
Day 11	7:24–8:10
Day 12	8:11–9:1
Day 13	9:2–29
Day 14	9:30–50
Day 15	10:1–31
Day 16	10:32–52
Day 17	11:1–33
Day 18	12:1–27
Day 19	12:28–44
Day 20	13:1–37
Day 21	14:1–25
Day 22	14:26–14:52
Day 23	14:53–15:20
Day 24	15:21–16:8

NOTES

Chapter 1: The End of the World as We Know It

1. Josephus, *The Complete Works* 3.6.12.

Chapter 2: Peace On Earth Goodwill to All

1. Austin Channing Brown, *I'm Still Here: Black Dignity in a World Made for Whiteness* (New York: Convergent Books, 2018), 175–76.

2. Marcus Borg and John Dominic Crossan, *The Last Week: A Day-by-Day Account of Jesus' Final Week in Jerusalem* (San Francisco: HarperCollins, 2006), 3.

3. Susan Ratcliffe, ed., *Oxford Essential Quotations*, 5th ed., online version, Oxford University Press, 2017, https://www.oxfordreference.com/view /10.1093/acref/9780191843730.001.0001/q-oro -ed5-00016497.

Chapter 3: Home for the Holidays

1. Matthew Desmond, *Evicted* (New York: Penguin Random House, 2016).

2. Robin DiAngelo, *White Fragility: Why It's So Hard for White People to Talk About Racism* (Boston: Beacon Press, 2018), 52–53.

3. Gordon Light, "Draw the Circle Wide," Common Cup Company, 1994.

4. Carol Kuruvilla, "Chilling Study Sums Up Link between Religion and Suicide for Queer Youth," *Huffington Post*, April 19, 2018, https://www.huffpost.com/entry/queer-youth-religion-suicide-study_n_5ad4f7b3e4b077c89ceb9774.

5. "Look Back at Oprah's Free-Car Giveaway," *The Oprah Winfrey Show*, original air date September 13, 2004, https://www.oprah.com/oprahshow/oprahs-entire-audience-are-surprised-with-new-cars-video.

Chapter 4: Hidden in Plain Sight

1. John Bell, "Carol of the Epiphany," *Sing the Faith* (Louisville, KY: Geneva Press, 2003), 2094.

Chapter 5: The Cradle, the Cross, and the Gift of Emmanuel

1. Douglas John Hall, *The Cross in Our Context: Jesus and the Suffering World* (Minneapolis: Fortress Press, 2003), 24.

2. Hall, *Cross in Our Context*, 40.

3. Sarah Klassen, "Incarnation," *Christian Century*, January 7, 2015, 12; italics in the original.

4. James Cone, *The Cross and the Lynching Tree* (Maryknoll, NY: Orbis Books, 2011), 158.

5. Scott Pelley, "Rejecting Hate, after Spending Nearly a Decade Spreading It," CBS News, aired December 17, 2017, https://www.cbsnews.com/amp/news/rejecting-hate-after-spending-nearly-a-decade-spreading-it/?__twitter_impression=true.